MARRIED TO THE SAS

FRANCES NICHOLSON

BLAKE

Published by Blake Publishing Ltd,
3 Bramber Court, 2 Bramber Road, London W14 9PB,
England

First published in hardback in Great Britain 1997

ISBN 1 85782 1661

British Library Cataloguing-in-Publication Data:
A catalogue record for this book is available from
the British Library.

Typeset by BCP

Printed and bound in Great Britain by
Creative Print and Design (Wales) Ebbw Vale, Gwent

1 3 5 7 9 10 8 6 4 2

Inside illustrations used courtesy of the author,
News International and The Defence Picture Library.

To Joanna

ACKNOWLEDGEMENTS

Thanks are due to my beloved husband for his encouragement and support in writing of my life with the SAS and my experiences with all the soldiers, their wives and their families.

I also want to thank my parents who have shown such kindness and understanding.

And especially, a big 'thank you' to all the wives and ex-wives of SAS husbands who provided the information for me to write this book, giving of their time and revealing their personal experiences and their innermost secrets.

CONTENTS

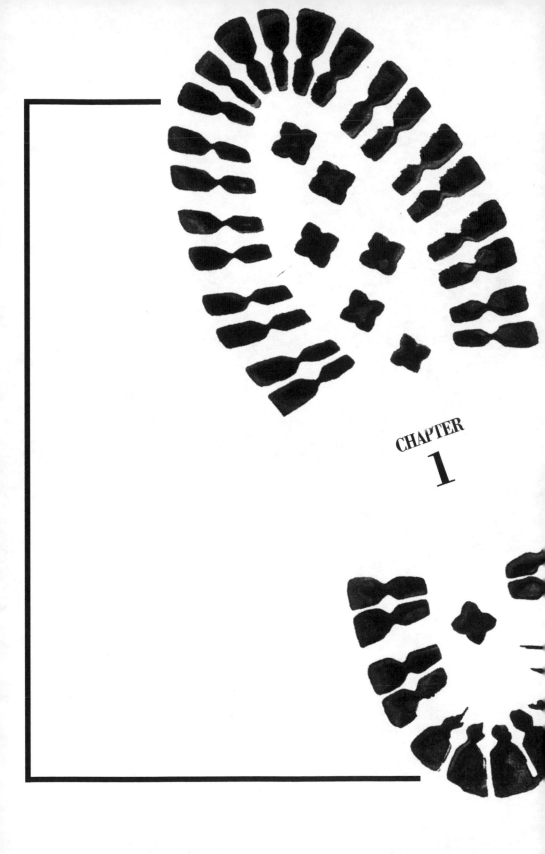

CHAPTER
1

'Strategic operations demand, for the achievement of success, a total exploitation of surprise and guile.'

COLONEL DAVID STIRLING,
FOUNDER OF THE SAS

IT WAS DURING LUNCH IN MAY 1982 that I heard about the SAS and I felt a chill down my spine. I was working as a supervisor of the restaurant at a management centre in Portsmouth and as I hurried about my work I heard the news flash: 'The Ministry of Defence has just announced that a Sea King naval helicopter with 30 SAS men on board has crashed in the Falklands. It is feared that as many as 20 men may have been killed.'

'What's the matter with you?' a friend asked as I quickly drank a glass of water, 'you look so pale.'

'Didn't you hear the news flash?' I replied. 'Twenty

of our lads have been killed in a helicopter crash in the Falklands. It just made me feel funny inside ... I don't know why.'

'Do you know anyone out there?' she asked, concerned.

'Yes, my brother Gary. He's a medic on the Canberra,' I told her, 'I must have thought he could have been one of those poor guys. But he's not SAS.'

In fact, I had never known much about the SAS before. And yet something had happened in that instant which I would never forget.

It would be two years later, on June 6 1984 — the anniversary of D-Day — that I had my first brush with an SAS soldier.

My father owned Nelson's, the famous 200-year-old inn in Gosport, Hampshire, which had originally been a smugglers' haven. I was helping out behind the bar. D-Day was a great occasion in Gosport and the pubs throughout the town were jostling with people reliving their wartime memories. But it wasn't only the old people who filled Nelson's that day.

I noticed a group of young, fit-looking men standing in the downstairs bar, throwing back pints of beer. I was told they had been there most of the afternoon and were staying at a nearby army barracks.

One in particular caught my eye. He was tall, good-looking and very well muscled. He also had the most beautiful blue eyes and a Mexican-style moustache. When he came to the bar to buy a round of drinks I suddenly felt vulnerable, as though I was 16 again.

Although I had met many good-looking young men,

none had affected me quite like this fellow. There was something powerful, dominant about him that set my nerves on edge. I was instantly attracted to him.

When he and his mates left the pub some time later I shrugged, believing I would never see him again and castigating myself for feeling so vulnerable.

Three hours later, I was busily washing glasses when he walked back in.

'Pint of lager please,' he said and, as I looked up, I saw him sizing me up, a smile on his lips. At first I didn't move.

'Pint of lager,' he repeated, a question in his voice and a bigger smile on his face.

'Oh, I-I-I'm sorry,' I stammered. 'Yes, of course, a pint of lager. Coming up.'

I blushed, grabbed a glass and pulled him a pint. 'That's 86 pence, please.'

'And what would you like?' he asked.

'I'm on orange juice, thanks. I never drink on duty.'

'Fine,' he replied, 'but you would occasionally have a drink after work I presume?'

'Yes, of course,' I replied.

'Good,' he said.

At that moment I looked at him for the first time, straight into his eyes. I knew what that remark had meant and I felt both embarrassed and excited.

Two hours later, I was driving my new friend to Portsmouth. We were going to have drink and to dance at Nero's night club on the promenade at Southsea. He had been asking me what job I had, about Nelson's and about my parents.

After some minutes of answering a barrage of

questions, I turned to him and said, 'Look, you've been asking me questions ever since we left the pub. Now it's my turn. What do you do?'

'Have you ever heard of the SAS?' he replied.

'Yes,' I said, though in truth I barely knew anything about it.

'Well,' he went on, 'we're based in Hereford ... that's near Wales, by the way. It's part of the Army.'

I knew that Hereford was near Wales and gave him a stony look as we parked the car. We dropped the subject.

Brian Pagnall was everything I had ever dreamed of in a man. That night he behaved impeccably — he took my arm as we crossed the road, opened doors for me, and stood up whenever I left the table. We danced and talked and we both felt we had known each other for ages.

Later, I dropped him off at Gosport barracks with a quick peck on the cheek, and I drove home.

At breakfast the following morning I asked my father what he knew of the SAS.

'What do you want to know?' he asked.

'Well, Brian, the man I went dancing with last night, is a member of the SAS.'

'He's what?' my father exclaimed. 'Rubbish!'

'What do you mean?' I said, flushing slightly, wondering why my father had reacted like that.

'There is no way, Frances,' he said, 'that a member of the SAS would pick up a woman in a bar and tell her on the first date that he was in the SAS.'

Warming to his subject, my father went on, 'I've worked with these men before, real SAS men. You will probably find he's a cook or something attached to the

SAS. But he won't be the real McCoy.'

I felt somewhat deflated and not a little annoyed with the man to whom I felt so attracted.

Brian was with a small unit of soldiers attending a navigational course at Gosport and during the next few weeks I came to know them all. We would all play squash together and I would chat to the others at the barracks. The more they talked, the more convinced I became that my father was wrong. They were SAS.

Ten days later Brian took me to London for the weekend. He took me to see the Changing of the Guard in Horse Guards Parade and he explained that he was in fact a Guardsman, seconded to the SAS. We stayed at a lovely hotel in Bray, near Maidenhead, with a garden full of daffodils. As a joke, he signed the hotel register 'Mr and Mrs Smith'. I wasn't even wearing a wedding ring. The receptionist simply looked at us and blushed, a big smile on her face.

I had no reason to feel nervous and yet I did. I felt awkward when we went upstairs to our beautiful, large room which, for some extraordinary reason, had three beds!

That was one of the most pleasurable nights of my life. Brian was a truly wonderful lover, so confident and so tender and loving, the passion magnetic. That night I experienced my first orgasm. The weekend seemed magical and I felt wonderful for days afterwards.

The following week, Brian was due to continue his navigational course in Torquay and he invited me to stay there with him. We rented a caravan and I watched him and the unit practising landings in the middle of the afternoon, dressed in their black wet-suits and coming ashore in their high-powered Gemini inflatables.

It seemed extraordinary that the SAS would organise such training in broad daylight in the middle of summer on a beach crowded with holiday-makers. Bathers were running into the sea for a swim while children built sandcastles — and the SAS men went about their highly secretive training!

I began taking photographs of the men and that night Brian was called in by the senior officer who asked that I should refrain from taking snaps on the beach — for fear of attracting attention!

The week with Brian was heavenly. We had a great time together, walking barefoot along the beach in the moonlight, visiting the local pubs and spending as much time as possible together, on our own. I even enjoyed cooking meals in the caravan.

Over the next six months, I would drive most weekends to Hereford in my ten-year-old Volkswagen after I finished work on a Friday night, a distance of about 130 miles. Three hours later I would collect Brian from Stirling Lines, the SAS camp, and immediately return to Gosport. On Monday morning we would stagger out of bed at 5.00am and I would drive Brian back to Hereford for 8.00am. Then I would return to Gosport, ready to start work at 11.00am.

It was exhausting, but I didn't care. I was enjoying the best days of my young life.

My parents treated Brian like a prospective son-in-law. They thought he was a great guy and gradually my father began to believe that he was, indeed, a member of the legendary force. My mother would cook wonderful meals for us and Brian behaved in the most impeccable way towards them, always treating them and talking about them with respect.

Only once did things go wrong. Within three months of our first meeting, Brian had told me that he wanted to marry me and he continued to protest his love, each and every day we were together. I wanted to believe him and I did. But Brian also told me that he wanted to behave correctly, to ask my father for permission to marry his daughter.

I thought that was wonderful and I respected him for it. We all arranged to meet for an evening drink in a nearby Hampshire pub. After the first round of drinks Brian explained everything to my father — how much he cared for me and wanted to marry me — and asked for his permission.

My father told Brian how happy he was at the idea and that he already thought of him as a future son-in-law. A toast followed, and then Brian went to buy a round of drinks.

As my mother 'Del' (short for Delphine) took a sip of her gin and tonic, she said, 'There's no gin in this drink.'

'I'm sorry,' Brian said, picked up her glass and returned to the bar with my father.

For two minutes, the manager, a stocky, strong-looking man in his 40s, insisted that he had put gin in the drink, and refused to add any more. 'Please, just put some gin in the glass will you?' asked Brian, expecting the manager to give in.

'Don't you try and tell me my job,' the manager said.

'If you want an argument, come outside, now.'

Brian walked over to our table and said to my mother and me, 'Excuse me, I'll be back in a minute.' And he walked outside.

Three minutes later, Brian returned to the table. 'We've got to go, now. I'll explain later.'

He looked composed and calm but I could see blood on his hands. I realised something had gone seriously wrong.

'Come on, Mum,' I said, 'I think we had better go.'

We jumped into my father's white Mercedes and he put his foot down, sending the gravel flying and creating a cloud behind us. As we drove away I could hear a woman shouting, 'They've killed my husband; there's blood everywhere.'

In fact, the manager had suffered a broken jaw and needed to wear a neck-brace for a few weeks. The police tracked down my father's car and Brian owned up to taking part in the fight. He was charged with grievous bodily harm and pleaded guilty.

The magistrate told him, 'You are a highly trained soldier, proficient in the art of unarmed combat who should not have attacked this man in such a way. We accept that you were provoked but you should have walked away from the situation.'

Brian was fined £200 and would later be fined again by 22 Regiment SAS for misconduct. Fortunately for him, the conviction would not be recorded on his military record.

Later, Brian told me, 'Now you know what I'm like. I would never have started that fight, I would never have challenged that man. But you saw what happened. He challenged me to a fight and I have never walked away from such a situation at any time in my life, and I never will. That's me. I'm sorry for what happened but that man asked for it. I hope you can understand.'

And I did.

*   *   *

Before Christmas 1984, we had booked our wedding at St Mary's in Alverstoke village, the church in which I had always dreamed of getting married as a young girl. I had known the church since my Girl Guide days.

One of the first questions the vicar asked us was, 'Have either of you been married before?'

'No,' I replied, smiling at Brian.

As he held my hand, Brian also replied, 'No'. I never thought any more about it.

One afternoon some days later, when Brian was on leave staying with my parents and me in Gosport, I returned home from my job in Portsmouth to be told that Brian had been seen, apparently drunk, sitting outside Lloyd's Bank in Gosport High Street at 3.00pm.

I ran to my car and drove along the High Street looking for him. I saw Brian slouching against the wall of the bank, looking as though he was about to fall asleep. 'What the hell are you doing?' I said, trying to haul him to his feet and put him in the car.

'I'm drunk,' is all he would say, 'I'm just drunk.'

As I tried to get him to the car, a policeman appeared. The officer behaved correctly, speaking politely and trying to help Brian to his feet.

As the officer put his hand under Brian's armpit trying to help him to his feet, I noticed Brian's attitude change. He jerked his arm away and I smelt trouble. Three times the officer warned him to get up, go to the car and go home, and three times Brian refused.

'You know I will have to arrest you, sir, don't you?' the officer told him.

'Fuck off!' Brian replied. 'Listen,' he went on, 'I'm a Sergeant in the SAS.'

'Oh yes, sir,' replied the officer, 'and I'm Mickey Mouse.'

He turned to me and said, 'I'm sorry about this, Miss, but I will have to arrest him.'

Another officer arrived and together they put him in the police car and drove away. His arrest, however, would have repercussions which I had never once considered.

After checking with the SAS headquarters in Hereford, the police released Brian into my custody and I told them I would get him back to Hereford before 9.00am the following morning.

On the car journey home a scared, contrite, slightly sobered Brian poured out his life story. He told me he would lose his job; that he would be thrown out of the SAS; that he would have to return to the boring life of a Guardsman. I tried to console him, telling him that many army Sergeants must have got drunk before without needing to quit the Regiment, but each time I tried to comfort him he would tell me, over and over again, that I didn't understand.

Finally, in exasperation I asked him, 'What? Tell me

precisely what I don't understand.'

'You know that name I have tattooed on my left arm,' he said.

'You mean Jenny?'

'Yes,' he replied, 'that's right.'

'Well?'

'Well,' he went on, 'Jenny's the name of my wife.'

'What?' I said, turning and looking at him, the man I loved so much.

'Yes,' he continued, 'and I have a daughter, a nine-year-old daughter. She has dark hair like yours and she could easily be *your* daughter.'

That remark flabbergasted me. I wondered what on earth he thought he was saying.

As we lay in bed that night, he told me that our relationship had to end; that he could not afford to get divorced, keep an ex-wife and a daughter and marry me, all on a Guardsman's salary.

Then he fell asleep, still suffering the effects of the alcohol. I stayed awake all that night worrying and wondering if it was possible to save our relationship, get married and live happily ever after. But each time I felt confidence returning, I felt I was only kidding myself.

When he awoke the next morning he didn't remember anything. He certainly couldn't remember what he had told me and so I slowly told him everything he had said. He stared at the ceiling, seemingly unable to take in just how much I knew. Not once while I told him what had happened and what he had said did he look at me.

'Listen, Fran,' he told me, 'I love you more than anything in the world; I want you to be my wife even if I have to start work as a dustman. I promise you we will be together.'

He told me that his divorce was going through and that he wanted us to live together in Hereford as man and wife, waiting to marry once his divorce was finalised.

I wanted to think he was now telling me the truth, but I naturally had my doubts. I didn't know what to think, but I agreed to take him back to Hereford, as I had promised the police.

Brian escaped with a warning and he persuaded me that I should move to Hereford, find a house to buy with him, and that we would live together until we could be married. He told me his divorce would be through in the spring and so we rearranged the wedding for July.

We found a little two-up, two-down at Bobblestock on the outskirts of Hereford. My parents bought us a three-piece suite, carpeted the house, and my mother made red and white check curtains for the tiny kitchen. It was my first home and I loved it. We even went to a farm outside the town and bought a lovely little black kitten we called Sam, even though Brian didn't like cats.

He behaved perfectly and I felt that we would be together for ever. We bought my wedding dress, an off-the-shoulder, full-length, white lace dress with a shoulder-length veil. I ordered the cake with the famous SAS winged dagger, as Brian wanted to be married in uniform.

Throughout the five months, however, I occasionally had my doubts that Brian was remaining faithful. Each morning he would cycle to work, leaving at 6.00am, and I wondered whether he was going straight to work or calling in to see his wife and child on the way.

And I wondered why Brian never wanted to go out

at night. I found a job working as a cashier in a local supermarket and would have loved to have gone out, at least at weekends, to have a drink, a meal or go dancing. He never wanted to, arguing that as he was away so much he preferred to have me to himself at home, where we could enjoy a quiet meal, drink a bottle or two of wine and make love.

It was shortly after our birthdays in June, when I was 26 and Brian was 28, that he came home one night to tell me that he had to leave for America the following day on a two-week training course. That night I dutifully ironed all his shirts and packed his case, and managed to cook an early dinner so we could spend the night together.

The following morning I kissed him goodbye, a long, lingering kiss, and went off to work. I phoned at around 11.00am to say a final goodbye but he wasn't there. At lunch I decided to go home, and the minute I walked though the front door I knew something was wrong. The house seemed almost empty and cold.

I went straight upstairs and noticed that his favourite print of three SAS soldiers, dressed in black, was missing. I checked his wardrobe and found all his clothes had gone. I ran downstairs and there was a note for me, explaining he had taken the print to be repaired because a small piece of the frame had been chipped.

But as I looked around the room, still confused, I realised that the photographs of his daughter, which he always kept on the TV set, were missing. Instantly, I knew beyond doubt that he had gone for good.

I felt hollow and lonely. I felt cheated and stupid and

angry at myself for refusing to see the signs. I went back to work, finished my shift in a daze and returned to my empty, rotten little house. That night I snuggled on the couch with Sam and stayed there, not eating or drinking and not knowing whether I wanted the phone to ring or not.

But it didn't ring, and in the morning I had a bath and went to work as usual at 9.00am.

The first person I met, another check-out girl, called across to me, 'Hi, Frances. I saw your old man in the pub last night.'

I heard the words, but I could not understand what she had said. He was in America, training, thousands of miles away.

'I think you must have been mistaken,' I said. 'He's in the States.'

'It was him, Frances,' she replied. 'He even came over and had a word with me.'

I felt awful, physically sick, for I knew he had lied to me. I knew I could never get through another day at the check-out. I made an excuse to my supervisor and went home.

The letter was lying on the mat inside the front door.

'Dear Frances ...' it began, 'I didn't know how to tell you this but I have taken the coward's way out ...'

He went on to tell me that he was, in fact, being posted to Ireland for two years and knew I would be upset. He begged me to understand and wrote how much he loved me. He urged me to sell the house and move back home to Gosport where he would come and see me when permitted home leave. He signed off, 'Love always, Brian'.

The phone rang as I finished reading the letter. It was my father who explained that he had also received a letter. 'What the bloody hell is going on, Fran?' he asked.

'I don't know, Dad. I'm just as confused as you are. I've just received a letter, too. I'll phone later.'

It would be one week later that I finally discovered the truth, when the wife of one of the NCOs came round to see me.

'Fran,' she exclaimed, a look of surprise on her face, 'what's the matter?'

'What do you mean?' I replied. 'I'm fine.'

'You've lost so much weight. Have you seen a doctor?'

'No,' I told her, 'I don't need to see a doctor. I know what the matter is. I've lost my man.'

She sat me down and began to talk. I hardly took in what she told me because I didn't really want to know all the sordid details. She said that Brian had returned to his wife and daughter; not, she explained, because he didn't love me, but because he felt he should be back with his wife and child. I didn't know whether to believe what I was being told, but as she spoke I realised that the love I had felt for him was draining away. Before she left later that evening I had determined that our relationship was over. Dead.

I thanked her at the door, said goodbye and told her I was fine. I went upstairs and stood on the scales. I had lost two stones in exactly one week.

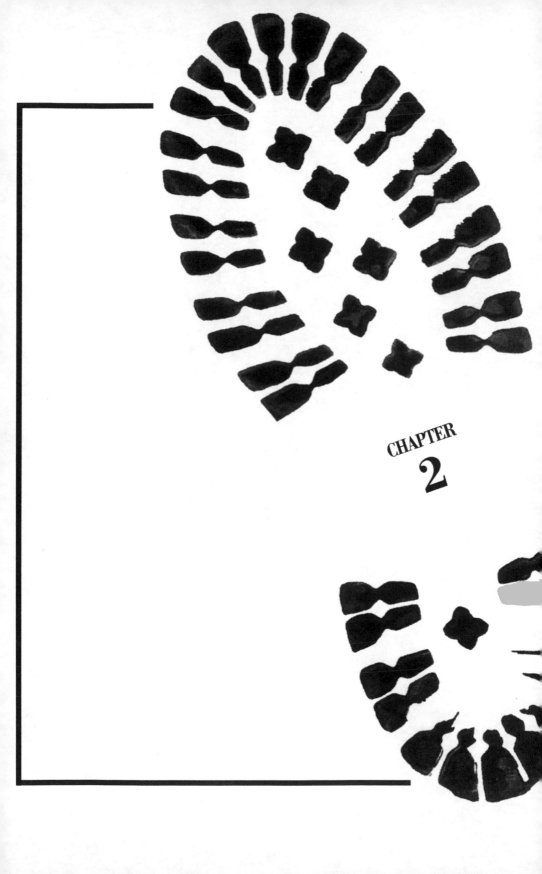

CHAPTER
2

'The bedrock principle of the Regiment was its organisation into sub-units of four men.'

COLONEL DAVID STIRLING

MY FATHER'S NAVAL CAREER as a sub-mariner ensured that I would be brought up as a true 'naval brat', moving from house to house every year or two, changing schools frequently and, as a consequence, suffering from a feeling of insecurity.

I was born on 3 June — Derby Day — 1959 at Hillingdon Hospital, Middlesex. Because it was Derby Day the nurses and doctors placed bets on whether I would arrive in the world before another expectant mother's child. At 1.30 in the afternoon I arrived, ten minutes before my unknown rival. My mother was convinced that I would always be a winner.

My father, however, did not know of my arrival for another 48 hours, because instead of the telegram being sent shore-to-ship, he only received the telegram when his submarine returned to its base in Faslane, Scotland.

Before going to school, my parents moved from Hillingdon to Helensburgh in Scotland for 18 months before going to Malta where my brother, Gary, was born in July 1961.

After returning to Tavistock on the edge of Dartmoor, we moved to Plymouth where I began my schooling in the autumn of 1963. Over the next ten years I would attend nine different schools, before my mother finally decided that the education of her two children was of paramount importance and they chose to settle in the Gosport area.

Even when my father was stationed at Barrow-in-Furness for two years they decided that the family should remain in Gosport.

I believe it was the fact that I changed schools so frequently that made me painfully shy. I found it difficult to communicate with other children or my teachers.

Whenever I moved schools I would deliberately keep myself to myself, never making friends with the other children in my class and wanting nothing more than to go home every afternoon to my mother.

At the age of six I attended a school in West London for just two weeks when I was staying at my grandparents' house. As I stood in the school playground, a girl came up to me, asked me my name and suggested we became friends. I knew I would only be staying there a few weeks and told her that I never bothered making friends with anyone because there was no point.

Indeed, I can hardly remember seeing my father during my young life. I knew he worked with submarines and that he spent most of his life away. I could tell when he was coming home because the whole mood of the house would change and my mother would seem on edge.

Like many young girls, I worshipped my father. I would wait at the front gate knowing he would be returning; knowing that he would walk up the garden path dressed in his naval uniform with his shoes highly polished and a big smile on his face. He would pick me up in his arms and swing me into the air before kissing me, and I loved him for that.

Even then I would beg him to put on his naval cap and I would love to wear it, too, as a special treat. I believe the fact that my father was in the services and wore a uniform would later make me somehow susceptible to men in the forces.

There may also be a link between my father spending weeks and sometimes months away from home, and the fact that I like being on my own, having the man in my life go away on trips, training exercises and short overseas postings. But not for more than a few weeks at a time.

I always wanted my father to be around when I started a new school as he gave me the confidence I desperately needed. He was there when I joined my secondary school, Privett Secondary School in Gosport. Although I felt embarrassed and awkward that day, it had nothing to do with him.

My parents insisted that I wore the regulation pleated navy-blue skirt which reached to mid-calf and flat brown school shoes. I carried a briefcase, rather than the school satchel I had pleaded with them to buy me. I felt frumpy, old-fashioned and convinced myself I looked foolish.

On the second day, however, I took matters into my own hands. I took another pair of shoes from home and would put those on as soon as I arrived at school. On the way to school, I would deliberately scuff the shoes along the road, trying to wear them out as quickly as possible so that I could then persuade my mother to buy a pair with heels.

As soon as I walked through the school gate, I would put down my briefcase and hitch up my skirt until the hem-line was mid-thigh. I even tried to lose my hated briefcase by deliberately leaving it on the bus one day.

Within two days the briefcase had been delivered back to the school. Stupidly, I had forgotten that my name was inside!

I enjoyed Privett. I worked hard, I liked the teachers, obtained good marks and even made friends with some of the other girls. Within a matter of months, I was even taking pride in wearing my school uniform.

In 1972, when the Government introduced comprehensive education, Privett was closed down and we were all moved to the local grammar school, Bay House School.

For me, and for many of my friends, that move proved a disaster which ruined my education and brought an end to any chances of gaining enough qualifications for a worthwhile career.

From the outset, the boys and girls from the secondary school were treated as second-class pupils. We were forced to discard our Privett School uniforms and wear the new comprehensive school colours — red, black, white and grey. The grammar school pupils continued to wear their uniforms of mid-green, with yellow and white. Of course they stood out as the privileged ones and we were made to feel inferior. We hated the concept.

And both sets of pupils refused to mix or even talk to each other. The enmity gradually became hatred and fights broke out, not only between the boys but also among the girls. Most of the cat-fights between girls would take place in the girls' lavatories, but much of the rivalry consisted of simply bitchy remarks and insults.

The chemistry teacher at Bay House walked into the classroom to take our first chemistry lesson and announced, 'I really do think it would be a waste of time to teach you children chemistry because I don't think you will receive any benefit whatsoever.' He looked around the class and then with a smile said, 'Instead, I propose to teach you a few card tricks and some card games. You'll probably enjoy that far more than chemistry.'

To a class of 13- and 14-year-olds, his idea seemed wonderful and we all happily agreed. During chemistry classes that year I learned card tricks, poker and three-card brag, and nothing at all about chemistry.

I was, however, considered bright enough to be admitted to the grammar pupils' maths class which was taken by the headmaster, but even he never made me feel at home, referring to the fact that I had been promoted 'from the other class downstairs'. I was allocated a desk at the very back of the class and, for most of the time, the headmaster ignored me. I had joined the class in the middle of the term but no one ever explained to me what I had missed.

As a result, I could not keep up but was not given any additional assistance. At one point, the headmaster asked whether I would prefer to return to the class below as I didn't seem able to cope, but I was determined to stay and struggle on.

In the last term, however, I had found my feet and with help from my father I passed the exam. I was thrilled.

I did not have so much success with my French, however, a subject which I loved. I really enjoyed learning a new language and worked hard to improve. I knew that my ancestors had fled to England from France in the 18th century and, as a consequence, I wanted to learn the language, and was determined to pass the examination with flying colours.

I would sit at the front of the class paying careful attention throughout the 40-minute lessons. I never missed a lesson and earned 'A's for all my homework. When my school report arrived, however, I had been given an 'F' for 'failed' and the report stated that I had hardly ever attended!

Distraught, I persuaded my mother to ask the teacher what had gone wrong. I had believed all along that I had a good relationship with the French teacher, a cheerful, slim, dark-haired woman in her 30s. But she told my mother that I never attended class and, worse still, confessed to not knowing who I was. My mother returned home in a determined mood, collected my school books and went back to the teacher.

'Have you never seen these books before?' she asked the teacher.

'Yes of course I have,' she replied, somewhat embarrassed. 'Now I know the girl you're talking about. She is very good, a wonderful student. I am so sorry, but I had no idea of her name.'

In a bid to extricate herself from such an appalling lapse of memory, my French teacher tried to explain that the forging together of the two schools had created great difficulties.

But it was too late for me to continue my French lessons, for the class into which I should have been placed had been filled. French, the one lesson in which I excelled, had been taken from me.

I felt miserable and angry and, as a result, I wanted nothing more to do with school or my education.

From an early age, I had intended to become an air stewardess because my aunt had worked for British Airways and had told me of the great life a young woman could enjoy flying around the world. She had told me that the airline would teach girls how to walk properly, do their hair, dress smartly and instil confidence.

I realised all to well that I needed confidence — I had been far too shy all my life. I hated myself — my 5ft 9in, thin, shapeless body, my thin knobbly-kneed legs, my long, lank, mousey hair and my size eight feet! At school I was called 'Wednesday legs' by the boys. They would shout to me across the playground, 'When's day going to break?' referring to my thin, straight legs. And, understandably, as much as I wanted to wear a bra, I never did, for I had no bust, neither did I have any sign of a backside.

I also discovered one day that I was one of the very few 15-year-old girls in my class who didn't have a boyfriend and had never had one. Naturally, I felt awkward, unwanted and unloved.

Worse still, my best friend, Marian, a lovely girl with long blond hair, blue eyes and a full figure, had a boy friend of nineteen! I was happy for her but also jealous. They were both kind to me, taking me with them on dates, inviting me to parties and going to the cinema. Desperately, of course, I wanted a boyfriend of my own.

She would also tell me the intimate details of their sex life, explaining what they did together and what it was like. She also revealed that she had been having sex since she was 14. I was surprised but not jealous, because I did not know what I was missing; I had never even been kissed by a boy!

That would change one night in the summer of 1975 when I was 16. For some months I had been watching one particular boy, aged 19, who would occasionally visit the Focus Youth Club at Lee-on-Solent.

Jason was dark-haired with brown eyes and small, handsome features. All the girls fancied him and I did, too. I would blush whenever he looked at me or even brushed past me.

As time drew on one evening, Jason had asked me to partner him in a game of darts and, fortunately for me, I was on form and my darts found their mark. He was impressed and asked if he could walk me home. I was embarrassed but happy, and readily agreed.

He suggested we take a short-cut to the bus stop and after walking for some minutes he stopped and began to kiss me. It seemed strange but I began to feel excited as he kissed my neck and stroked my thigh. He suggested we lie down on his jacket and I readily agreed. He undid the zip of my trousers and tried to rip them off. I tried to stop him but he continued, pulling as hard as he could as I fought to stop him.

'Don't you want me to do this?' he asked, surprised.

'No, no I don't,' I said.

He tried to reassure me, telling me everything would be fine, that he knew what he was doing and that he wouldn't hurt me.

I suddenly felt scared and screamed 'No!' Then he clamped his hand across my mouth, stifling me. But my scream had made Jason realise that I wasn't enjoying his attentions.

'I'm sorry,' he said, removing his hand from my mouth. 'I thought you wanted me to.'

'No,' I said, the tears running down my face.

Then, mockingly, he asked, 'Don't tell me you're a virgin!'

'Yes,' I told him, 'I am. There are still some of us about, you know.'

'I'm sorry,' he said, looking embarrassed. 'Let me help you up. I'll walk you to the bus. Let's just forget it, OK?'

'That's OK with me,' I replied.

I would hear later, however, that Jason had no

intention of 'forgetting it'. After seeing me to the bus stop, he had returned to the club and told his mates of his latest conquest.

I did, though, enjoy one sweet teenage relationship with a wonderful guy, who treated me with gentleness, as though I was someone special. It was through Iain, a blond, blue-eyed, well-built young man four years older than me that I began to gain confidence for the first time in my life.

We met on holiday in Wales and I spent four days with him, becoming the closest of friends without ever even kissing. We remained friends for the following year, even though he lived 160 miles away in Nottingham.

We wrote to each other every week and would occasionally see each other but the relationship was doomed because of the distance between us. That relationship, however, gave me the confidence to begin holding my head up and enjoy my life.

I had taken the advice of my aunt and a career's adviser to further my education and study some different subjects at Highbury Technical College in Portsmouth. I decided to take a two-year course in hotel management, which I was told would be most useful in securing a job as an air stewardess. My father had quit the Royal Navy in 1978 and decided to open a pub in Gosport. He asked me whether I would consider working with him rather than joining an airline, so I went to the Isle of Wight to gain work experience in hotel management for a summer season.

After starting work in Nelson's, my father's first pub, I met Jack, a handsome young bricklayer in his early 20s who had a reputation for always being in trouble, fighting and brawling most Saturday nights. But he had the great looks that girls adored, and was tall, strong and athletic with wavy, swept-back hair. He reminded me of a young Clint Eastwood.

Though my parents did not totally approve of the relationship, we spent two years together. Most weekends I would stay at his home with his divorced mother, sharing his bed — a tiny, rickety, noisy single bed — which embarrassed me greatly as his mother could hear every movement, every conversation and every murmur through the paper-thin walls.

I would walk down to breakfast unable to speak to her or look her in the eye because I was so conscious of the fact that we had dared to make love in her house, even though our efforts in that area were naïve and, generally speaking, short lived, lasting no more than a couple of minutes.

Our life together quickly became rather boring, because Jack's idea of indulgent behaviour was a few pints of beer at the pub, a few hands of darts and watching his favourite football team, Portsmouth United, every Saturday afternoon. On Saturday evenings he wanted to go drinking with his mates, persuading me to stay at home with his mother watching television. He would arrive home some time around midnight, happy and half-drunk and then want to give me the time of my life, an exercise in the missionary position, leaving me embarrassed as well as frustrated.

I could never persuade him to take me to the cinema, out dancing, or to any parties. We never went out to eat, except for the occasional beefburger and chips which we would eat walking along the street. Occasionally he would take me for a drink in the pub, but for never more than an hour. The routine never varied and I would wonder if this was what couples called 'married bliss'. I could not imagine that life would always be so dull, and I never got the slightest enjoyment from sex. At that time I became convinced that sex was one of the most overrated activities, simply a way of making babies. In retrospect, I would be amazed that I stayed so long with Jack, but there seemed no way out of the relationship.

One night, however, I seized my chance. One Saturday he returned home drunk with a love-bite on his neck and I challenged him about it. He told me it was nothing, just a bit of fun. He tried to persuade me to go to bed with him but I refused, telling him to sleep off his drunken state on the couch while I went to bed. The following day I was still determined to leave him.

'Don't leave me,' he pleaded.

'Listen,' I told him, 'you've obviously found a new girlfriend and you never show me any respect.' I went on at him, telling him in no uncertain terms how boring life had become for me and that I was only 21.

'Please don't go on,' he said. 'I've a surprise for you.'

'What surprise?' I demanded.

'Come with me,' he said, 'and I'll show you. Please.'

Reluctantly I agreed, and he drove me to a new housing estate in Gosport Town. He showed me a lovely two-up, two-down little house.

'So what?' I said.

'It's ours,' he replied, 'I bought it for you as a surprise.'

I was flabbergasted. He had never even suggested we move into a house and settle down. He had always seemed so happy living with his mother, having his food prepared, his clothes washed and ironed, a place he could treat as a hotel with no questions asked. His purchase of the house had shocked me and I felt awful. But I knew that a long-term relationship with Jack would never work. I had to get away from him and live a fuller life, enjoy myself and investigate new horizons.

So I walked away, left my father's pub, found a new job as a supervisor running the restaurant at the Portsmouth Management Centre, and moved back home with my parents. I was 22 and felt I had barely lived. Girlfriends I had known from school seemed to be having far more fun, far better relationships and enjoying their jobs and their lives, while I seemed to have stagnated in a boring relationship with a handsome bloke.

Each morning I needed to take my shower by 6.00am, to make sure I was at work by 8.00am. I would finish work at 2.30pm, stay at the hotel and take a two-hour nap before starting work again at 6.00pm, finishing at 10.30pm.

I would then change out of my rather severe white blouse and black skirt, take a quick shower and drive to a private club in Southsea where I worked in the cocktail bar. It wasn't all work at the club. I was encouraged to drink and dance with the members and I made a number of new friends, but I was not permitted to finish until 3.00am, when a few of us left for breakfast at the local casino. I would be asleep at home by 4.30am. Ninety minutes later my alarm went off. Somehow I kept up this pace for nearly a year, sometimes even helping out my dad at weekends by working in his pub.

I would never work so hard again in my life, but I loved it. I spent the money on holidays and clothes. Never before had I had any money to spend on myself as my parents had always restricted my pocket money, telling me that I didn't need to waste money on clothes. I wasted plenty of money on clothes during that year, and I never regretted a single penny.

Happy, adventurous and enjoying my new-found freedom, I was vulnerable and open to anything — even to meeting a man and falling in love. Then I saw Brian in my father's pub and my extraordinary life with the SAS began.

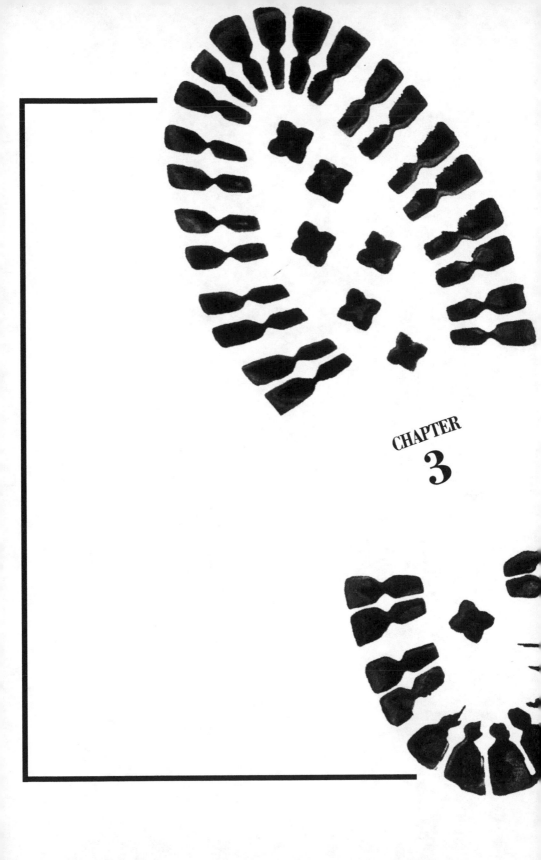

CHAPTER
3

> 'The number four was deliberately chosen
> to avoid the emergence of a leader
> in the orthodox sense.'

COLONEL DAVID STIRLING

AS I LOOKED AT MYSELF IN THE BATHROOM MIRROR and realised that my affair with Brian was finally over, I determined that I needed to kick-start my life again. I would leave Hereford and find a job elsewhere.

The following morning I bounced out of bed for the first time in weeks, dressed quickly and walked to the local paper shop around the corner. I collected the two local newspapers and returned home. Over a pot of tea, cornflakes and toast I scoured the situations vacant, ringing the possibilities with a pen.

I saw one advertisement for a manager in the White

Swan, a family-run restaurant. I phoned, spoke to the owner and was invited for an interview the following day. As I drove through the beautiful countryside in the heart of Worcestershire, I simply knew that this job would be for me.

I immediately took to the owner and his wife and the rest of the staff appeared friendly and unfussy. They seemed to want to take me on, showing me a lovely room which would be my living quarters, and telling me of their attitude to a successful hotel business, combining friendliness and a relaxed atmosphere with a quiet efficiency.

Two days later I drove back to Worcestershire to start my new life.

I enjoyed the work, the ambience and a great rapport with the staff who were all prepared to help each other out. The owners, too, were a delight to work for. From the outset we felt part of a team rather than employees, and I saved all the money I made, though it wasn't very much. I kept the money in a biscuit tin in the wardrobe and every few weeks would count it.

Two months after I moved to the hotel I realised why I was so keen to save my money when I had so enjoyed spending every penny so much when I had been earning a healthier salary only a year or so before. In my heart I knew I wanted to return to Hereford.

I would lie awake at night thinking of the city, the places I loved to visit, the men and women I knew and those I wanted to keep as friends.

For some extraordinary reason I couldn't keep Hereford out of my mind and it began to worry me. I would think of the men I knew there and I realised that I hardly knew anyone really well, except Brian, and he had proved to be a failure.

And yet something was drawing me back there, and I knew I was saving enough money for me to return and live the sort of life I wanted in an atmosphere where I had always felt an underlying sexual tension, an air of expectancy and excitement.

I began returning to Hereford whenever I had a few days off. I would take the train from Worcester and the moment I arrived at Hereford station I felt as though I was home, a sensation that excited me.

I would stay at a girlfriend's house and we would go shopping in town. I would feel happy but with a nervousness in the pit of my stomach, a sexual awareness that kept me on edge, an anticipation that I would meet someone. I would feel the spring in my step, my body slightly taut, even though I was back in the place where I had endured so much unhappiness.

Sometimes we would go for tea and cucumber sandwiches at one of the hotels; at other times, we would go to Saxty's for a glass or two of wine. We would return home for a nap before dressing for a night on the town. Though my body tensed in anticipation wherever we went, in my heart I never wanted to meet anyone, preferring to sit and watch what was going on, observing, not daring to talk to anyone in case I should find them attractive.

One weekend I met Charlie, a Signals guy attached to 22 Regiment, who had been RTU'd (Returned to Unit) that week for a drinking and driving offence. He offered me his small, terraced house for the incredible rent of only £100 a month! I vaguely knew the house and accepted the offer before even stepping inside. I knew it to be a great bargain and he seemed happy for me to rent it.

I returned to Worcester thrilled at the prospect of returning to Hereford. I wasn't so happy, however, at having to quit my job, feeling guilty because everyone had been so kind to me during my three months' stay. But I had no alternative. I knew I was being drawn back to Hereford like a magnet, and persuaded my employers to let me leave almost immediately. As I returned on the train with all my worldly possessions packed in a couple of suitcases, I felt I was going home.

It was imperative for me to find a job to pay the rent. I also needed to find someone to take the spare room in my house to help with the rent and provide me with some spending money.

The first weekend I met a taxi-driver, Paul, who was looking for a room. He moved in almost immediately. My first priority had been achieved.

I found a job in a chicken processing plant and began meeting new friends. I enjoyed the simple pleasures of life, just walking along Hereford's streets, window-shopping in my favourite stores and soaking up the atmosphere. I just knew that something would happen in Hereford, something that would alter my life for ever, and it did.

After only a few days I could pick out the Regiment men at 200 yards. Nearly all would be wearing the unofficial off-duty uniform, Gortex or Helly-Hanson mountaineering jackets, blue jeans, desert boots and a Bergen (back-pack). And, at that time, most also sported the obligatory Mexican droopy moustache.

Even if an SAS man was walking away from me, I could tell if he was Regiment because of his confident walk, striding out as though he owned the place.

I had only been back in Hereford a matter of weeks when I met Ken in Oliver's, then the 'in-place' to dance and drink at weekends. I was sitting on a stool at the bar when he came over and asked me what I would like to drink.

'A Bacardi and Coke,' I replied.

'With ice and lemon?' he asked, making sure I realised he was a sophisticated young man.

Ken was short, barely 5ft 7in tall, and as I sat on the stool I knew he didn't realise I was a good couple of inches taller. I didn't want to leave the stool for fear of towering over him and frightening him away. Little did I realise that he knew I was tall and, indeed, it was one of the reasons why he approached me. He would eventually marry a girl more than 6ft tall.

Ken was a northerner with a great sense of humour who loved the outdoors, going for long walks in the country in all weathers and driving along narrow lanes in his old, open-top Triumph TR6.

He loved to surprise me, arriving at the door with no invitation and wanting to stay with me all day and all night, persuading me that I had no need to go to work or keep appointments that I had arranged days before. He also occasionally surprised me by collecting me from work, but I would never know when he would arrive at the factory gates.

He wanted to sweep me off my feet, but I didn't want a serious relationship because I was still scared about what had happened with Brian. Ken was fun to be with and I enjoyed his company, his sense of adventure and his spontaneity. I also quite enjoyed driving around the country, visiting lovely old pubs in his noisy sports car.

Not knowing where my young life was heading, I was persuaded by a couple of girlfriends to see a clairvoyant they knew by the name of Madam Edy. She had read tarot cards and palms for a number of women at work, and they had all been impressed.

I had never been to a clairvoyant before, but decided to see what she might tell me. Perhaps I saw her because I needed some hint, some suggestion as to what I should do with my life, what I should do about a career and, more importantly, where I should settle down. I also hoped that she might give me a clue as to my future love life, hoping that she could see a partner with whom I could enjoy life and settle down.

Madam Edy came to the house early one September evening, and over a glass of wine she talked to me for more than an hour.

By the end of our time together, she told me that I was an emotional 'roundabout', and that my love life would always be on a roller-coaster. She saw that my future would not be hard, that I would have most of the good things of life, but that there would be a price to pay, an emotional penalty.

She told me not to fret or worry about my future for

within three months I would meet a man with very bright blue eyes, though she warned me that I would have to be careful.

Three days later, I answered the door bell and, to my surprise, Brian was standing there.

'Hi,' he began in a breezy fashion, as though he was the next-door neighbour asking to borrow a cup of sugar.

'Hi, what?' I answered, glowering at him and wondering what on earth he was doing on my doorstep.

A little taken aback, he said, 'I was wondering if I could come in and have a chat.'

'What about?' I asked, not yet fully opening the door.

'I'll tell you in a minute.'

'Alright,' I said, naturally curious as to what he had to say.

As he stepped through the doorway he said cheekily, a big smile on his face, 'Stick the kettle on, make us a brew.'

As I walked into the kitchen I knew there had been no change in Brian. He was the same as ever. As I filled the kettle and put it on the hob I knew that I still fancied the bastard. He had been the first person with whom I had really enjoyed a warm relationship and the first person with whom I had enjoyed a full-blooded sex life.

As we sat sipping our mugs of tea, I said, 'Well, tell me, what are you doing here? What to you want?'

'I just wanted to see you,' he said, 'I happened to be passing and wanted to see how you were getting on.'

I knew that was rubbish, because he lived with his wife and child on 'the patch', the name the SAS lads gave to the married quarters near Stirling Lines.

'Oh yes,' I replied, my voice deliberately sceptical, determined to give him a hard time.

As the conversation continued, I knew that Brian was not visiting me on a goodwill mission, but seemed to be trying to find out whether I would consider having another go at our relationship. He seemed to be hinting that that was what he wanted, but I would not be tempted that easily.

'How's Jenny?' I said. I knew asking after his wife would annoy him.

'Fine, fine,' he replied, trying to change the subject.

'Still together then?' I asked, although I had seen them walking past McDonald's in Hereford only 48 hours earlier.

'Yes, yes,' he said, obviously desperate to end the conversation.

'Does Jenny know you're visiting me tonight?' I asked, tongue in cheek, knowing that his wife was still at work that evening.

'She knows where I am 24 hours a day,' he said, warming to the subject. 'I can't go anywhere without Jenny knowing all my movements and the people I'm meeting.'

'Good,' I said, 'that should help keep you in check. It might even save a few broken hearts.'

'What do you mean?' he asked, searching to see whether I would give him a sign, any hint that I still loved him.

'You know what I believe, Brian — once bitten, twice shy.' And I looked him in the eye wondering how he would reply.

'Listen,' he said, 'You know I loved you very, very much. You know we had a great time together and you must understand that I haven't been able to get you out of my mind ever since we split.'

I looked at him, wanting to believe him, but my look clearly showed that I doubted his real motives.

With a big smile he said, 'Come on, Fran, let's go upstairs, you must remember how good it was.'

I knew all right. I remembered very well, but I was not about to tell him that. I was tempted, but I made myself remember the heartache I suffered when I found out he was a married man with a child.

'Are you sure I can't tempt you?' he asked, almost pleading.

'Out, you dreadful man,' I said with a big smirk on my face. 'You know you should be at home with Jenny not here trying to race me up to bed.'

He agreed to leave and asked whether he could pop round at some future time for another cup of tea.

'Yes, of course you can,' I said, hinting that I would love to spend two or three hours in his arms.

Before he opened the door and stepped into the autumn night he kissed me on the cheek. 'You're great,' he said. 'You know I still love you.' Then he was gone.

I had been tempted but knew that to return to a wild affair with Brian would be stupid. 'Damn him,' I thought, 'how did he know I was feeling lonely and vulnerable?'

But I knew I had to put him behind me. It had been Madam Edy who had told me that I would soon reach a fork in the road and would have to make an important decision. She had been right and I knew I was right to send him away, despite the fact that he had been the only man in my life I had truly loved.

*   *   *

In December 1985, I went as usual with a group of girls to the Regiment's private night club inside the camp, The Paludrine, named after the anti-malaria pill all soldiers took daily when in mosquito-infested areas.

As we walked into the club just before midnight, I saw a young man with long hair and a deep sun-tan standing alone against a wall, a pint of lager in his hand. I also noticed that he had the most incredible, piercingly blue eyes.

One of my girl friends asked him, 'Why aren't you at home?'

'I fancied a few pints before going home,' he explained, not moving from the wall.

'But you've only been back a couple of hours.'

'Yeah, I know,' he said, taking a long draught from his lager. 'But I needed a few of these first.'

'What a pig,' I remarked to Jackie, one of my friends, as we walked away.

'Oh, he's always like that,' she said. 'That's McNab; he thinks he's God's gift to women. Whatever you do, Fran, stay clear of that man.'

'With those eyes I should imagine he can have anyone he wants,' I said, and thought nothing more about him.

A week later I was walking down High Town, the

pedestrianised centre of Hereford, when I saw a young man striding towards me. From the way he walked I could tell he was Regiment, and then I realised it was McNab, the bloke I had met at the club.

I tried to avoid his gaze and looked into the shop window as I continued to walk towards him.

'Hi,' he said, stopping me in my tracks, 'we met last week at the club.'

At first I feigned surprise, pretending not to know who he was, but he persisted.

'Don't you remember?' he asked in his Cockney accent. 'We met in the club. I was having a quiet beer and you kept staring at me.'

'Yes, of course,' I said. 'I'm sorry, I didn't recognise you.'

Little did he realise that the reason I had been looking at him at the club was because I thought he was arrogant and selfish. I had also noticed that he was dressed like a waiter, in white shirt and black trousers.

'Fancy a brew and a sticky bun?' he asked. 'I'm just going to have one.'

'Yes, that would be nice, thanks.'

We sat drinking coffee and tea for more than an hour. Andy McNab tucked into a ham sandwich, a doughnut and an apple turnover but, despite pleas and gentle pressure, he failed to persuade me to eat anything.

'I hate eating on my own,' he said, 'please eat something. Be a sport.'

'Thanks, but no thanks,' I said, determined that I would not eat anything, simply because he wanted me to.

The more we talked, the more I realised that under all his bravado Andy was rather a nice bloke, and more shy than he appeared. But I didn't like his arrogance and wondered why so many men under 6ft tall always seemed to be rather big-headed.

He gave me a lift home. As we pulled up outside my front door, I said, 'I would invite you in for another cuppa but I've got a pile of ironing to do before I can hit the town tonight.' I was looking for an excuse.

'Oh, fine,' he said, as though unperturbed by my reason for not inviting him inside, but he didn't sound very convincing. 'I've a friend who lives right around the corner. I'll pop in and see him.'

As arranged, I met three girls in a Hereford pub that evening and, after a few Bacardis, we decided to visit Oliver's, a nightclub with a cocktail bar upstairs and a very noisy disco below. It was also the place that the Regiment blokes frequented, mainly on the look-out for girls. Every girl was aware, however, that the SAS men who went there could be single or married, separated or divorced, and it was often difficult to tell the difference.

Most of the SAS fellas stayed together in a group of perhaps ten or twelve and, usually, they would have a drinks kitty. Invariably they would be downing pints of beer or lager. It would only be later in the night that they would switch to shorts.

They also had a very poor reputation among the girls for being extremely mean with their money. It was more a hard fact than a standing joke that SAS men never bought a woman the first drink.

I was advised by a girlfriend, 'If you want to catch an SAS fella the golden rule is that you have to buy him the first drink. It's their bravado. They all think they're God's gift.'

As I ordered drinks for my girlfriends at Oliver's that night, I felt a tap on my shoulder.

'While you're there, get us a pint of lager,' the voice behind me said. I turned and saw Andy standing there with a great grin on his face.

'Cheeky bastard,' I thought, but by then I did think he was rather cute. 'For your cheek I will get you one,' I said.

When I walked over to the group of blokes where Andy was drinking I heard him say, 'This is how you train them fellas,' and he laughed as he took the pint from my hand. He winked at me, trying to be friendly, but I had overheard his rude comment. I determined that I would never buy the little runt another drink in my life.

An hour later, as I was drinking alone, not wanting to dance, Andy walked over to me with a glass in his hand. 'I think I owe you a drink,' he said, handing me the glass.

'Thanks,' I said, but I knew that I would have much preferred an apology. I also wondered why he had bought me a Jack Daniels whisky when I was drinking Bacardi rum.

Within minutes the slow, smoochy music had begun and I found myself dancing happily with Andy. He chatted to me as he held me close and I began to enjoy his jokes and his little comments about other people which made me laugh. The more we danced, the more relaxed I became and the antipathy I had felt towards him drained away.

As we left the dance floor, one of his close friends from the Regiment, whom everyone called 'Johnny Two-Combs', came up to Andy.

'Where's my Jack Daniels?' he asked.

Andy looked at me and grinned, knowing that he had been caught out. 'I'll go and get you one,' he said, and Johnny and I chatted as we waited for Andy to return.

We returned to the dance floor and spent another hour locked in each other's arms. I began to unwind, to feel relaxed as this man, whom I hadn't liked very much, talked softly to me, giving me confidence and a feeling that I had known him for months.

We walked home together having been unable to find a taxi. It was a cold December night and when the rain began to beat down, I wondered why we hadn't waited in Hereford for a cab.

Forty minutes later, soaked through, we arrived at my home and I asked him if he wanted to come inside to dry off.

Rather sheepishly, he replied, 'Well, I would prefer to be inside rather than face another 40-minute walk back to Hereford.'

I made him a sandwich and brewed a pot of tea as we sat in front of the gas fire and talked. He asked me to show him my photograph albums and I let him see my life, my parents, our homes, our holidays and my brother Gary.

After 20 minutes I felt that he now knew my entire life.

Under most circumstances, I would have kept my family photo album hidden from the prying eyes of a new boyfriend until we knew each other well, but with Andy it seemed natural that he should want to know all about my earlier life and I didn't mind him asking me a thousand questions about everything and everyone he saw in the photos that night.

And yet throughout that evening he never talked about himself, his life, his childhood, his family, the Regiment or, more importantly, about his wife, for I knew he was married but separated from her. Whenever I asked him a question he would answer only obliquely. I felt he was avoiding answering any questions directly as though he didn't want me to know anything about his life. That worried me, so I decided to be more forthright.

'Where's you wife?' I asked him bluntly.

The question obviously took him by surprise. 'What do you mean?' he asked, playing for time.

Sensing that he was, once again, avoiding the issue, I repeated the question, this time making a joke of it: 'Your wife, remember, the girl you married?'

'We're not married,' he said in a straightforward, matter-of-fact voice, as though he was telling me the time, 'we're getting divorced.'

'Oh yes,' I replied, with as much sarcasm in my voice as I could muster.

'It's true ... honest,' he said, raising his right hand as if swearing on the Bible. 'I promise you.'

He didn't like this conversation one jot. 'I think I'd

better go,' he said, taking offence at my jibes. 'It's obvious I'm not wanted here,' he said, seeking sympathy. 'I'll find somewhere else to stay the night.'

I should have let him go there and then. I should have opened the door and encouraged him to walk off into the cold, wet night. I should have let him march straight out of my life and then my involvement with Andy McNab would have been over and done with in one short night of drinking and dancing.

He looked at the unpleasant weather outside. 'Can't I stay here,' he asked, 'in the spare room?'

At that moment the tough, cock-sure SAS man who would become a national hero during the Gulf War seemed utterly exposed. I felt I had been too hard-hearted. I didn't really know anything about his love life; I didn't know whether he was living with his wife or whether the marriage was over.

I told him that he could stay the night in the spare room because my lodger friend was away for the weekend and I knew he wouldn't mind.

'Do you fancy a glass of wine?' I asked him. 'I've only white.'

'If you have a bottle, yes,' he replied.

As we sat in front of the fire drinking, only once did Andy kiss me. When he reached to pick up his glass from the floor and our eyes met, he kissed me on the lips, gently and quickly, as though embarrassed. Thirty minutes later I knew it was time for bed and I showed Andy to his room, and I went to undress in mine.

Two minutes later there was a tap at the door. 'Come in,' I called, and he pushed open the door and stood there with a pleading look in his eyes like a spaniel wanting to be taken for a walk.

'Yes?' I asked, smiling back at him.

'I just wanted a goodnight kiss.'

'Just one,' I said and he walked in, closed the door and began to kiss me.

When I awoke the following morning and saw Andy lying beside me I burst into tears, angry with myself for permitting him to stay the night and make love to me when I had no respect for him.

I knew that he would now return to the camp and tell the lads that he had scored once again, and it made me feel cheap and awful. Over the previous evening I had had no intention of sleeping with this arrogant man and yet, five hours later, I had happily gone along with the kissing and love-making.

'Why are you crying?' he asked. 'What's the matter? Did I do something wrong?'

Between the tears I told him, angrily, 'I had no intention of sleeping with you. And I have to tell you that of all the people I could have chosen to sleep with last night, you would have been the last person on my list. I don't even like you. And what makes it all so dreadful is that you're still legally married.'

'We'll talk another time,' he said, eager not to let me start attacking him again as I had done the night before.

He kissed me goodbye, a quick peck on the cheek, and told me he had to go to camp. He would return later. There was, of course, no way that I could ask him why he had to return, for I knew he would say that he could tell me nothing of his work. As I saw him walk down the path, I convinced myself that that would be the last I would ever see of Andy McNab.

I would learn quickly enough that the alleged secrecy of their SAS activities was used throughout the Regiment to hide whatever nefarious activities they got up to. It was, of course, a perfect cover for their numerous illicit love affairs, as their wives and girlfriends never knew from day to day, or even hour to hour, what their men were doing or where they were.

Every wife of an SAS soldier, every girlfriend, knows that their men have the opportunity to have affairs, misbehave and act in the most outrageous fashion and all beneath the cloak of secrecy.

Most wives know that it goes on because the SAS men themselves tell the wives and girlfriends of their mates, men in their own Squadrons, that so-and-so is having an affair, cheating on his wife, playing away from home, or whatever. And yet we were all meant to believe that our man was the only honest Joe in the entire Regiment, the only faithful one, not playing up, not messing about and never for one moment having an affair with another woman!

But every wife and girlfriend also recognises that the men of the Special Air Services undergo the most rigorous, constant training of any Special Forces in the world. They realise, too, that their men are prepared to put their lives at risk carrying out whatever task is assigned to them. They also know they fly to distant parts of the world to undertake dangerous missions which, more often than not, are life-threatening.

And that is why the men of the SAS are so special, so different, almost unique in their appeal to women, especially women searching for someone sexually exciting, who want to share in some small way with the adventurous spirit, the carefree attitude and the danger and glamour of their lives.

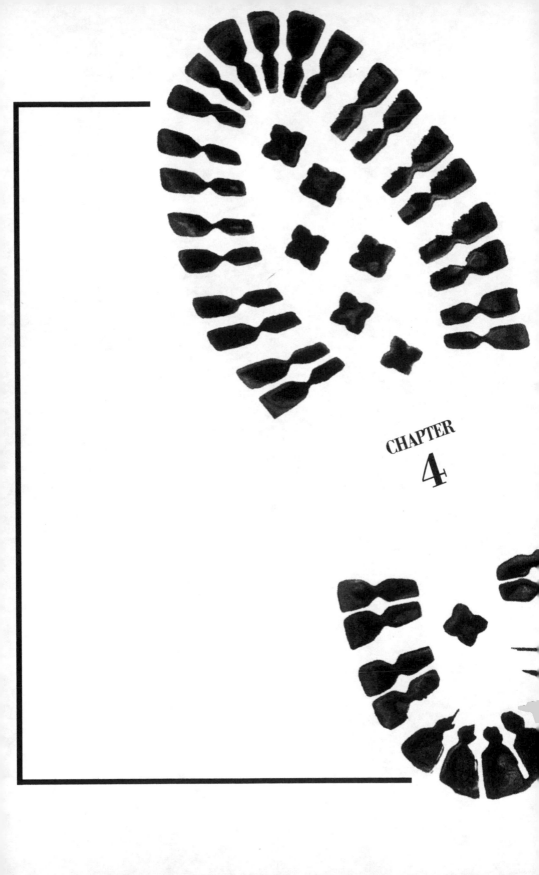

CHAPTER
4

'The ruthless selection of soldiers who motivate and discipline themselves virtually eliminates the risk of obedience breaking down.'

COLONEL DAVID STIRLING

THAT AFTERNOON I WAS LOOKING through estate agents' brochures strewn over the sitting-room floor. My parents had offered to put a deposit on a small house in Hereford so that I could settle down, rather than move from house to house every few months, constantly searching for suitable rented accommodation.

My mind was miles away, wondering whether I did, in fact, want to live entirely on my own, cut off in a small house, or whether I would prefer to move into a large house with other young single women for company.

I was shaken from my thoughts by the sound of a car outside.

I wondered who was visiting me and never, for one moment, thought it would be Andy. I looked out of the window and saw him walking up the path, holding a Tesco carrier bag.

My heart leapt as I walked to the door to let him in. 'Hi,' I said, trying to sound nonchalant, but my heart was beating fast. I wondered if he had forgotten something from the previous night, or if he had a message for me, or whether he really had returned to see me and be with me.

At first I didn't feel so wonderful when he told me that he had recently bought the house next door and intended moving in some time in January. Cheekily, he added, ' I thought it would be a good idea if I got to know the neighbours better.'

Without letting me say a word, Andy went on, 'I thought we could have a quiet night together,' handing me the Tesco bag and looking up at me for my response. I had ideas of a romantic dinner for two in a restaurant somewhere in the Hereford countryside, rather than the dish of Tesco's Chicken Curry from a tin-foil tray which I could see in the bag. But he had also included a bottle of French Bordeaux red wine.

I shouldn't have been so critical, because the evening was wonderful. Andy was brilliant, chatting non-stop, cracking jokes, laughing and making me feel great. We enjoyed the bottle of wine and then drank another bottle I had in the fridge. And the curry tasted good as well.

That night I had no arguments with Andy. The more we talked the more involved I became and the more I realised I had been unfair in condemning the man out of hand, pre-judging him when I had no real evidence on which to base my attack.

I wanted to believe everything he told me; that he had left his wife, that they were planning to divorce and, as he kept repeating, that he was a free man once again, free to love someone else. As it turned out, all these claims were true.

As I sat there listening to him chatting away, I knew I wanted that 'someone else' to be me. I wanted to be the object of his attentions and I wanted to make love to him that night.

I went upstairs and brought down my large, warm double duvet and we made love for hours in front of the gas fire. I wished it could have been a lovely big, open wood fire, but that would have to wait. And he was great.

As we lay together under the duvet, Andy talked of his plans for the future, our future. He talked of leaving the SAS, making a fortune, of a large house in the middle of the English countryside and of the two of us and, hopefully, a daughter, spending the rest of our lives together. It sounded wonderful, fantastic, unbelievable and I wondered if he was dreaming a dream too many.

The following day, Andy moved most of his clothes and his personal items into my house and that weekend we went to the married quarters where he had lived with his second wife, Debbie, and cleared out everything. The quarters had to be immaculate before the Army would accept the hand-over, so we spent the day scrubbing and cleaning the entire house.

While Andy was upstairs, the bell went and my good friend, Lisa, was on the doorstep.

'What are you doing here?' she asked, taken aback.

'Helping Andy clear up,' I replied. 'Why?'

'Well, I heard he was moving out,' she replied, 'and thought I would come and lend a hand.'

Then she suddenly stopped and her mouth fell open. 'You're not ...' she began, 'you're not *seeing* him are you?' she said, a sound of utter disbelief in her voice.

'Yes, I am actually,' I said, 'he's moving in to my place.'

'For God' sake,' she said, sounding bossy and concerned, 'come outside. I want to talk to you.'

We had hardly taken two steps outside when Lisa turned on me. 'What the hell do you think you are doing? I warned you about this fucking man. You know he's still married, don't you? And now he's moving in with you. He's been married twice, he's had God knows how many affairs around this place and now you're giving him a roof over his head. You need your bloody head examined, Fran, you really do.'

I was taken aback at first by the tone of her voice and the force of her argument. I knew Lisa was only this angry out of concern for me, but I didn't want to hear her slagging off Andy in such a ruthless fashion.

'Listen,' I heard myself saying, 'he's not that bad, you know. He's not some dreadful ogre.'

'You don't know what you're doing,' she said, annoyed with me.

'Lisa, please listen,' I pleaded. 'I'm 26 years old. I'm

no longer a kid; I know what I'm doing ...'

But she wouldn't let me finish. As she stormed off, she shouted to me, 'Don't tell me I didn't warn you, Fran. Do you hear me now? Don't say you weren't told.'

As I walked back inside, Andy came down the stairs. 'Who was that?' he asked.

'Your 'friend' Lisa,' I said. 'She doesn't think it's such a good idea that you move in with me.'

'Why not?' he asked.

'She called you a male slut, if you really want to know.'

'Charming,' he replied, 'that's really sweet of her.'

As we continued cleaning the house, I tried to put aside everything Lisa had said. I just hoped that she was wrong and that my instincts wouldn't let me down, but I remembered the lies that Brian had spun for so long and how I had believed everything he had said.

Andy had told me he liked the fact that I called him by his first name. 'No woman has ever called me by my first name,' he said at the time, 'they all called me Mac, as everyone does in the Regiment.'

It was while I was cleaning the kitchen that I found a calendar on which Debbie had written notes. Every entry began with the name 'Andy'. I should have realised then that this man was already prepared to tell me lies and he hadn't fully moved into my house yet!

We spent Christmas 1985 together in my Hereford house and, without a doubt, it was the happiest Christmas of my life.

We went shopping together, bought the Christmas dinner together and I insisted on having all the trimmings including the Christmas pudding. Andy brought over a crate of wine and we bought each other little presents which we wrapped and opened together on Christmas morning, but only after we had spent an hour in each other's arms.

It seemed extraordinary that before Andy and I had ever been out together he had put down a deposit on the small two-up, two-down house in Haston Close, Hereford, the one next to mine!

And together on 2 January 1986, we spent the day moving all my clothes and personal items from the house I had rented for six months into Andy's next door. When the last item, the kettle from my kitchen, had been moved in, Andy opened a bottle of champagne and he made a toast.

'To us,' he said and we clinked glasses and kissed. We looked around the house, deciding how to decorate it, what colour schemes to choose, what we needed and what we would do to the place.

'Don't you think we should have central heating?' I asked, 'because my house was freezing and this will be, too.'

'We won't need central heating,' he said, laughing, 'you've always got me.'

I hoped to persuade him to change his mind some time later because I knew that he would be away on training exercises from time to time and I didn't fancy living in a cold home all winter. Sure enough, later that year Andy happily paid for a heating system to be installed, but only in the bedrooms.

Two weeks later, Andy was on a course in Salisbury,

learning how to load and fire the American Stinger ground-to-air hand-held missile launcher and he wanted to go and meet my parents who lived nearby in Hampshire.

'I want to meet your parents at their home,' he told me. 'I would prefer to meet them on my own to see if they like me. If they don't like me, too bad, but I would prefer to see them alone so they can judge what I'm like. I don't want them to think that all SAS men are like Brian, telling lies and leading girls up the garden path.'

From the outset, my mother loved Andy. 'He is charming,' she told me, 'absolutely lovely, and Andy and your father got on really well. I can see why you like him.'

Andy, too, enjoyed meeting my parents and especially visiting my father's pub in Gosport High Street. On his return to Hereford, Andy was full of the trip. 'Your father let me go behind the bar and serve the customers. I was introduced to everyone and they were all so kind. And they all love you, darling; they think you're wonderful. Some of the regulars told me how they missed you serving occasionally behind the bar.'

Andy told me how my parents had spoilt him throughout his stay, giving him lovely meals and waiting on him from breakfast to dinner-time.

One evening a few weeks after we moved in, Andy returned home from work to announce that he was going to Botswana in southern Africa for a few weeks. He explained that the Regiment had been invited to take part in exercises in the swamps.

I understood that Andy would have to go away from

time to time, sometimes at a moment's notice, but that didn't upset me because of my childhood experiences. I had been used to the man in my life, my father, being away for months at a time and I had learned to enjoy his company when he was around and make sure I didn't miss him too much.

I never considered my father to be in any danger, really. It seemed perfectly normal that people, like submariners, live for months under the sea. With Andy, of course, it would be different and not because he was my lover.

I realised that the SAS were sent to trouble spots and faced real danger, and people in Hereford would frequently talk about the possibility of one or two men not returning from a trip. They took it for granted that danger went with the job.

I was advised by the wives of some of the men that one of the most important lessons to learn quickly was never to have a row with your man before he was due to leave on an exercise or, more importantly, an active service mission. And they would stress that because they knew that when their husbands were about to go overseas, the tension would mount, making it all too easy for pathetic little problems to be blown out of all proportion.

I took that advice to heart and would learn to hold my tongue whenever Andy was about to go away, even though I felt myself becoming touchy, wondering if he would be OK and whether he would return wounded. But I never permitted myself to worry that he might never come back, that he might be killed in action. If, for one second, that thought flashed across my mind, I would deliberately cast out the idea as unthinkable. In that way I hoped I wouldn't worry when he was overseas on a mission.

But, of course, my determination sometimes wavered and I would become anxious, but I never told Andy. That, I knew, would be unfair to him, so I kept those thoughts to myself.

I determined to keep myself busy. I had my job five days a week working in the factory, and had made a few friends. My father occasionally came to Hereford to keep me company and happily carried out little DIY jobs around the house, because I thought it would be great for Andy to arrive home and be able to sit around and relax, rather than have to worry about the mundane jobs that needed attention around the house.

But I had made two errors. I hadn't realised that after many exercises the SAS men are taken off to a plush five-star hotel out of harm's way, where they rest and recuperate in total luxury, arriving home looking sun-tanned and really fit, the privations and dramas of the tough training exercise all but forgotten. I also never realised that Andy was looking forward to returning to his little house in Hereford, and planning to do all the little jobs my father had carried out.

Andy was away for a few weeks in Botswana and I enjoyed receiving his letters, full of affection and, rather surprisingly, hints about a possible baby.

In one letter, Andy wrote that he was sitting by the edge of a swimming-pool watching a young father playing in the pool with his baby son, and suggested that we should think seriously about having a child. As I expected, however, he wrote nothing of the training exercise, except when one of their Gemini inflatable boats was attacked by a hippopotamus while the troops were making their way along the Okavango waterways. No one was injured, although the hippo ripped a hole in the Gemini, causing chaos for everyone on board.

Whenever Andy returned from a few days or a few weeks away, it would be like a wonderful honeymoon. He would arrive rested, fit and relaxed and wanting to spend the first day or so in bed, making me feel fantastic and helping me to appreciate how fortunate I was to have such a good relationship. But these honeymoons would not last more than three days.

Indeed, among all the SAS wives the three-day honeymoon became a standing joke, and we would laugh at what would happen on the fourth day after the men returned to Hereford.

Generally, the day after one of our 'honeymoons', Andy would decide to check the house and garden, and especially the bills and bank statements. It seemed that, no matter how perfect I tried to make everything before his return, none of the work that I had carried out would be praised or even commented on. However, the one or two jobs I hadn't completed would be pointed out and I would be made to feel incompetent, useless and idle.

The one job I hated was mowing the lawn, and when Andy returned he would always complain that the lawn needed cutting. I told him that I couldn't mow the lawn using an old-fashioned, dilapidated manual mower with blunt blades, so he bought an electric Flymo so I wouldn't have any further excuses.

But I still disliked mowing the lawn. Even to this day I hate mowing lawns and don't consider it a woman's job. I would always leave the lawn mowing to the last minute and neighbours would comment to me that Andy must be on his way home simply because I was cutting the grass. But that was a risky business because, more often than not, it would rain the day before Andy returned and I would be unable to mow the blasted tiny piece of grass.

He would never know it, but on some occasions when he was returning suddenly from Northern Ireland, I would be out and mowing the lawn at 7.00am, before driving to Heathrow to pick him up.

I wasn't the only one. Most of the wives would complain that all the work they had carried out during their husbands' enforced absence would receive scant acknowledgement, but their men had an uncanny knack of always finding the one job that had not been completed.

What the SAS men never accepted, however, and something which caused friction between many couples, was the fact that the men maintained when the women, alone at home, had to take decisions, they would generally be the wrong ones.

They didn't seem to understand that decisions had to be made immediately on any number of matters, especially if the man was away for several months; nor would they accept that their partners would desperately want to make the right decision and would worry about doing so.

It seemed that the men wanted to find fault on their return, perhaps to show their importance in the marriage and to ensure that family life revolved around them and their rôle as head of the household. Unfortunately, the rows that followed would sometimes end in blows.

Quite often, a few days after an entire Squadron returned to Hereford, one or two women would be seen walking around the town wearing sunglasses, and it had nothing to do with bright sunlight.

Understandably, some of the SAS men would become jealous of their wives and girlfriends. Their womenfolk understood that the jealous types believed that they were going out on the town, visiting night clubs and having affairs while they were away, whether there was any evidence to suggest it or not.

Amanda, a dark-haired, attractive, petite friend of mine would be forbidden by her husband, an SAS Sergeant, from going out without him at night. I would arrange to see her for a drink and a chat and maybe a meal in a restaurant, whereupon he would go berserk, despite the fact that it was only a girls' night out.

She told me that she became alarmed when he became so angry one night that when she had dressed to go out he ripped the telephone cord from the wall and tied her up so expertly she could not move for three hours, by which time it was too late to come and join us. The marks on her arms and legs were visible for days.

What angered her even more, however, was the fact that after he had tied her up and left her lying bound on the floor, he told her he was going out for a few beers with his mates. He returned somewhat the worse for wear and, as he untied the cord, he said, 'I hope that's taught you a lesson.'

She talked to other SAS wives who had problems with their partners, all apparently infuriated that their wives should want to go out on the town on their own, without their husbands. Most believed the real reason the men wanted them to stay at home was because so many SAS blokes sleep around with other women whenever the opportunity arises.

Emma, an attractive blonde in her 30s who had been married for ten years, would frequently be seen around Hereford suffering from heavy bruising around the face and neck. She had been called 'Four Eyes' at school, teased all her life for having to wear glasses and, at a little over 5ft tall, had difficulty in defending herself against the unwanted attentions of her 6ft husband, a muscle-man proud of his physique.

One day she came round to my house in floods of tears, her face heavily swollen. I could see the start of bruising on her face and knew it would develop into two serious black eyes.

'The bastard,' she sobbed over and over again. 'He's started hitting me again.'

I could see that she was holding her ribs and asked where he had hit her. 'All over ... my stomach and chest and everywhere,' she continued. 'Usually he only gives me a few slaps, but this time he was real nasty, vicious. I'm sure he wanted to hurt me.'

I tried to persuade her to go to see the SAS Families'

Officer, the person responsible for sorting out family problems such as wife-beating. 'I can't do that to him,' she said, 'he'll get into the most awful trouble and I wouldn't wish that on anyone.'

She told me how her husband would promise not to beat her in future and how, every month or so, he would lash out at her, often for no apparent reason.

'I've been a good wife to him, you know,' she went on. 'I've given him everything he ever wanted but I can't keep putting up with all this.'

Emma would eventually leave her husband and return to her home town in the north of England. Many ex-wives of SAS personnel are encouraged to move away from Hereford, back to their origins, rather than stay around, a reminder of broken marriages. Most SAS wives believe the reason ex-wives are encouraged to disappear is to give the blokes a free hand to start again and live the life they want with no hassles and no embarrassing baggage.

I would see Emma shortly after her divorce came through and before she left Hereford for good. She told me how happy she was to be leaving the place.

'It's brought me nothing but trouble, this place,' she said. 'My old man would accuse me of having affairs all over town with so many fellas. If I kissed one at a Christmas party he would tell me I had been sleeping with the guy.

'But he wasn't that bad, really. The day our divorce came through we had a celebration. He asked me if I would fancy a quick one for old time's sake and within two minutes we were in bed together again like the old times.'

One night I was having a quiet drink with a girlfriend in The Paludrine, when an SAS man, whom I had known casually for some months, came up to me and asked me to have a drink. For more than 30 minutes he chatted away, with the conversation becoming ever more risqué. Later, in front of his wife, he had the audacity to invite me out to dinner.

'Just the two of us,' he said, conspiratorially. 'I'll leave the wife at home, no one will know.'

But I was convinced that she must have overheard.

I looked at him, inspecting him from the top of his head to his shoes, and without saying another word, I left the bar stool and walked away.

'I felt insulted that he should think I would want to go out with him in the first place, and felt totally embarrassed for his wife, having to listen to her husband making propositions in front of her. As I walked away, I noticed her looking at me as though I had encouraged her man.

'In fact, I had been trying to end the conversation for some minutes, because I felt uncomfortable being chatted up by this married man with his wife looking on.

Wives living in the married quarters would tell of overhearing the most dreadful rows, even though they might be living three or four doors away. Sometimes they could hear screams and yells followed by silence, but no one would ever dream of intervening or phoning the Ministry of Defence police. The great majority of the marital problems of SAS personnel, however, would filter around the camp and would never be brought to the notice of higher military authorities.

And most of those rows erupted over money or other women.

Members of the SAS are among the highest-paid soldiers in the British Army, and the great majority of their wives work as well, whether doing part-time or full-time work. The houses around Hereford were not expensive compared to many areas of Britain, and much of the family income would go on clothes and enjoying a comfortable lifestyle, going out eating and drinking.

SAS men were notorious for having fads and happy to spend their hard-earned money on the current fashion — it could be the latest haircut; expensive, high-powered Japanese motorbikes; leather jackets; 501 jeans; or, as was the case in the late 1980s, Armani suits which they nicknamed 'the Gucci look'.

'Johnny Two-Combs', a member of B Squadron, a short, blond-haired man who took pride in being a champion dancer, liked to believe that he was the fashion idol of the Regiment. He would always dress expensively and immaculately and would love to stand in a bar and show people the labels of his jacket, his shirt, his tie and even his shoes!

Many SAS men laughed at Johnny whenever he sported a new fashion and yet, within three months, scores would have adopted the same look though they may not have spent quite so much on their kit.

When a particular fad was introduced to Hereford, the majority of the soldiers would want to follow suit, no matter how much the latest gimmick cost. They didn't seem to realise that they were slavishly following someone else's ideas rather than opting for individuality.

An argument broke out in a bar one night when someone suggested that the SAS were all clones of each other, prepared only to follow fashion rather than have the courage to be themselves and adopt their own characteristics and fads. The argument didn't end in a fight but one or two SAS men seemed on the point of throwing a punch.

Perhaps I was fortunate, but Andy never laid a finger on me whilst we were living together, nor did he ever threaten me. I can also say that I was never tempted to hit him, but there were some SAS wives I met who, when roused sufficiently, would attack their husbands — sometimes in public.

At an SAS Troop dinner party at the Merton Hotel in Hereford, one wife took umbrage at a remark her husband made at the dinner table. The wine had flowed all night and most of us were half-cut, when I suddenly heard a crash at the end of the table and everyone fell silent.

At the far end I saw one of the Sergeants sitting bolt upright with red wine pouring down his head and face and on to his clothes. His wife, angry at a disparaging remark he had made about her boobs, had picked up a bottle of wine and smashed it over his head.

For a few seconds, everyone was silent and then there were roars of laughter, one reason being that the Sergeant was bald and the wine made it look as though he had a head of hair again.

He also saw the funny side. As the wine dripped

down his face he sipped it into his mouth until he realised it wasn't wine he was sipping but his own blood — the bottle had cut his scalp open.

Sometimes, Hereford would seem more like a cauldron than the home base of the famous SAS. The passions and tensions among the élite troops would cause serious problems for so many families.

To many wives it seemed that the Regiment was far, far more important than the personal happiness of their married officers and men, their wives and their children.

Andy and I were happily, madly involved, but from the very beginning of our wonderful relationship I feared for our future together.

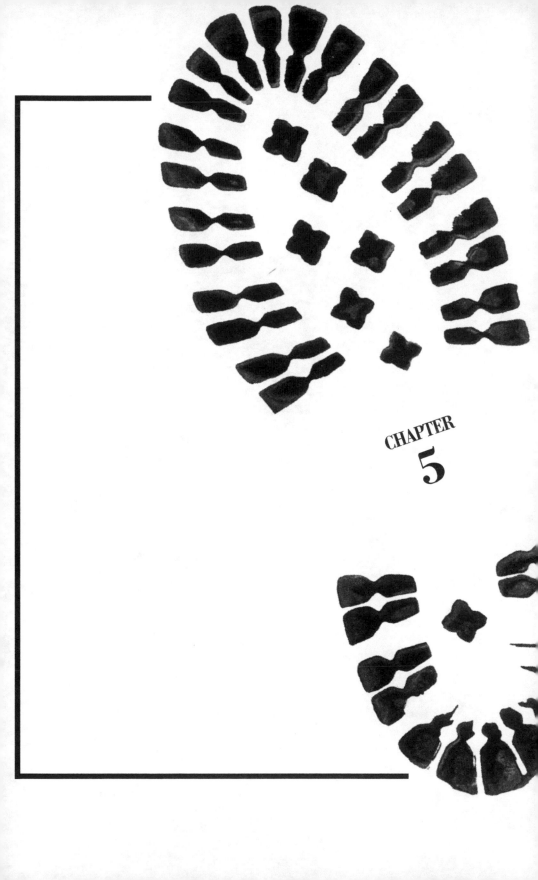

CHAPTER
5

'Expulsion from the SAS becomes the only sanction which a member really fears.'

COLONEL DAVID STIRLING

FROM THE VERY BEGINNING OF OUR RELATIONSHIP, Andy seemed keen to start a family. We would see young babies being pushed in prams or toddlers walking around the supermarket in Hereford and he would make cute remarks, hinting that he was looking forward to becoming a father.

As we strolled around holding hands, Andy would frequently say, 'I'm ready to start a family. I've found the woman with whom I want to have a baby and I think we should go for it.'

It seemed strange that Andy, a tough SAS soldier

whose life was always demanding and often dangerous, should so want to start a family within weeks of our first meeting.

'Are you always like this?' I would ask him, wondering if he had been as keen to start a family with his two previous wives.

'I've never been like this with anyone else in my life,' he said. 'It's because I love you.'

It seemed difficult to understand, but I would tell him that it was lovely and reassuring to hear him tell me how he felt towards me.

Andy had been married twice before. At the tender age of 18 he married Christine, a girl two years older than him. He would tell me that Christine, from Lewisham in South London, was a 6ft tall, beautiful model with long blond hair, who regularly appeared in the pages of *Vogue* magazine.

Andy explained that the marriage had broken down primarily because of his commitment to the Army. Andy was then in the Green Jackets, based at Tidworth in Wiltshire.

He told me that Tidworth was 'a God-forsaken little runt' of a town which held no interest to a young bride used to the glare of photographic lights, the sophisticated social life of London's top models, and a highly successful career. He would spend months away serving in Ireland with the Green Jackets and Christine became bored and resentful.

At the end of one tour of duty in Ireland he returned home and Christine issued an ultimatum, 'It's me or the Army, Andy.'

He told me that he chose the Army for both their sakes.

Andy told me that he met his second wife, Debbie, a petite, attractive girl with blond curly hair, at a disco at RAF Wroughton, near Swindon. He said that, although they had known each other for six or seven months, they decided to marry after he was posted to Germany with the Green Jackets.

As a Corporal, and if married, Andy would be entitled to quarters in Germany and so they married in August 1982, shortly after the Falklands War.

Andy and Debbie settled in Germany where she found a job in a local military hospital and she learned to speak fluent German. But Andy told me that he became bored with the Army and decided to seek selection for the SAS.

He spent months preparing himself, training to peak fitness for the summer selection in July 1983. But he failed because he managed to get lost during a map-reading exercise.

Back in Germany with the Green Jackets, Andy was even more determined that he would have another crack at SAS selection at the first opportunity, in six months' time.

This time he passed, and within a matter of weeks he was flown to Brunei in the Far East, his first overseas mission with the Regiment.

He told me that his life had become so hectic and he became so selfish that he and Debbie drifted apart. In reality, his second marriage had lasted little more than 18 months.

I talked to Andy about his relationships and his

marriages because, although we had only been together a matter of weeks, he was happily discussing having a family.

I feared that he might not be the type of man who would want to settle down, change the baby's nappy, or be prepared to sit up all night with a little one. I also feared that he might prefer to be out with his mates, visiting the Hereford night spots rather than staying at home with a tired young mum and watching television.

The more he talked of having a baby, the more concerned I became. And yet he could not have been more attentive, more loving and seemingly more involved than I would ever want from a man.

I believed Andy absolutely. He would tell me about his early life and I knew he hated and resented the fact that his birth mother had him adopted at a very early age. His adopted mother told me later that Andy had been handed over to her at six weeks, and that he had never known his natural parents, although he did know that his father was Greek and his mother English and that they had met in London.

During those early months together, we wanted nothing more than to be with each other and Andy proved a wonderful, loving man who was fun to be with. Only once did we have a humdinger of a row and that was over a former relationship which he knew nothing about.

I was cooking dinner one night in the spring of 1986, when Andy stormed into the house, slamming the door behind him. He strode into the kitchen and his face looked like thunder.

'What's the matter with you?' I asked, half jokingly. 'Had a bad day at the office?

'You never told me about Ken,' he shouted.

'What do you mean?' I asked, somewhat confused.

'You went out with him, didn't you?'

'Well, yes,' I said, 'but that was months before we had even met.'

'Don't you know he's got a reputation as a womaniser?'

'Hasn't half the Regiment?' I said, trying to make the matter as light-hearted as possible, keen to take the heat out of his violent temper.

At that he just walked out of the back door. I continued making dinner and an hour later he returned, walked in and kissed me, somewhat unexpectedly, on the cheek.

'I'm sorry,' he said, 'I love you so much. I can't think of you going out with any one else, ever. It burns me up thinking you've ever screwed another man.'

*   *   *

The more time we spent together, the better and deeper our relationship became and the more positive I felt towards Andy. I, too, began to think it might be rather lovely to have a family of our own.

Deep down, however, I feared that I might never be able to conceive. When I was 19, my family doctor had told me that I might have one of my Fallopian tubes blocked and could have problems conceiving. I had never been on the Pill or used any other birth control and yet I had never become pregnant.

I told Andy all this and we went for tests at a Hereford clinic. There, the doctor told me that my fertility level was normal and she could see no reason why I could not conceive, unless one of my tubes was not functioning properly. She suggested that I should consider having a 'D and C', but not make any decision for some time yet.

Andy also agreed to have a sperm count at the clinic and was handed a specimen bottle. He was told to go into a small room and produce some sperm. After five minutes, he poked his head round the corner, showing me that the bottle was still very much empty.

'I can't ...' he said, 'I can't do anything in this room. Do you think they might have some porno magazines or something? I need help.'

The nurse heard Andy complaining and came to have a word with me. 'If he's having problems, you could pop in and give him a helping hand ...' and laughed quietly as she walked away.

I went and knocked at the door. 'What is it?' he shouted.

'It's me,' I said, 'do you want me to come and help?'

'No ... I'm fine ... go away,' he said, 'I'm nearly there. I'll be out in a minute.'

A few minutes later he emerged with a big grin on his face, happily waving the bottle. 'That was very nearly impossible,' he said, 'until I began to think of you in your suspenders.'

'Ssshh,' I said, blushing madly because the nurse must have heard everything he said.

We both tried to make light of the whole episode, but I could see that Andy was worried by the possibility that he might be suffering from a low sperm count. He joked and laughed about the clinic, but he was also taking the matter far more seriously than he pretended. 'If I am firing blanks,' he said, 'there's nothing they can do to help, you know that.'

'Let's wait and see the results,' I said, trying to reassure him. 'There's no point in worrying until we know the facts.'

'OK,' he said, 'let's go and have a drink and a bite to eat and go home for a cuddle.'

Andy had been told to phone the clinic 48 hours later when they would have the results. That night he could hardly sleep, so concerned had he become that the count might be worryingly low. He woke me at 7.00am and begged me to make the call.

'I don't want to know,' he shouted. 'If it's not what I want to hear, for God's sake don't tell me. OK?'

The clinic told me that Andy had no problem — his sperm count was normal.

When I returned to the bedroom, Andy McNab was hiding under the duvet, his hands over his ears, fearful that I would be bringing bad news. I stood there laughing and he turned and looked at me, saw I was laughing and said, 'Well?'

'Well,' I repeated, 'you're normal ... normal!'

'Outrageous,' he said, 'outrageous. Come here, you lovely girl,' and within seconds he was back to being the Andy I knew and loved.

Two weeks later I discovered I was pregnant, and

Andy was determined to try and establish the exact moment of conception. We became convinced that it was after one of our famous games of chess.

Andy and I liked playing chess together. He hadn't played the game before and I taught him. He mastered it quickly, but because I had the greater experience I would usually win.

For fun, I devised a game of strip chess. Whenever a chess piece was taken the other one had to remove an article of clothing. And it didn't matter if you lost a king or a pawn.

Andy happily agreed to the rules, so before we started I ran upstairs and quickly pulled on another five or six layers of clothing.

'That's not fair,' he exclaimed when I came downstairs again, as he was only wearing a T-shirt and jeans. 'I want to win this game.'

'Andy,' I told him, giving him a kiss, 'you'll not be disappointed. I think we will both win.'

'That's alright, then,' he said and we sat down to play.

The pawns disappeared quickly, and so did our clothes, but to make the game more interesting we opened a bottle of sparkling wine and after each piece was taken we clinked glasses and took a large gulp of wine. Before all the pieces had gone, the bottle was empty. So Andy, dressed in nothing but his socks, padded out to the kitchen for another bottle.

I had lost most of my clothes and I couldn't wait any longer so I followed him into the kitchen. As I put my arms around Andy's waist he opened the fridge and took out a can of cream. He shook it and then turned and

All dressed up… Me, 1997.

Our Wedding, 1987. A wonderful day.

Top: Speech! Speech! Andy takes up the challenge on our Wedding day.
Below: Hold me close… Our Wedding day.

Top: Andy and I at my brother's wedding, August 1988.
Below: Pregnant! Andy proudly points, 1986.

Andy, off to the office, 1989.

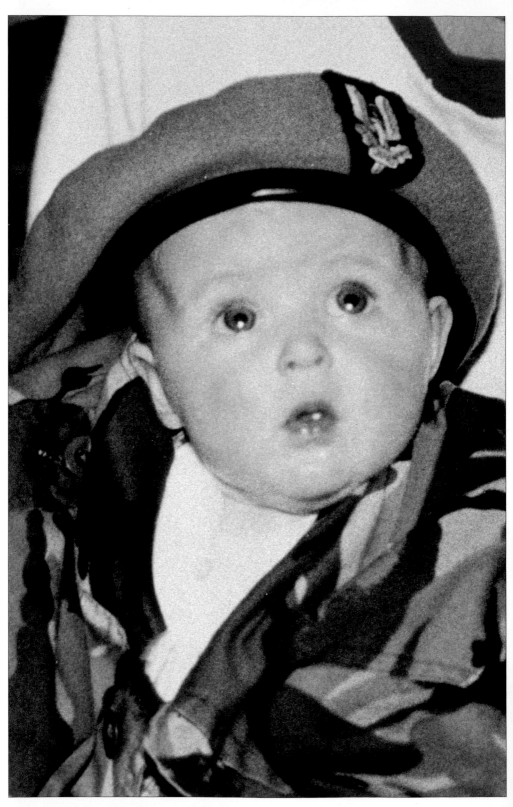

'When I'm older, can I join the SAS?' Jo, 1987.

Andy and Jo in the Brecon Beacons, Summer 1989.

Top: Andy holds Jo … just back from Nepal, May 1987.
Below: Armed and dangerous, November 1994.

squirted the cream all over my chest, legs and stomach.

'Don't move,' he implored, 'I've always wanted to do this to you.' And he began to lick the whipped cream from my body. But he never finished the task and within minutes I was sitting on the kitchen work-top with my legs wrapped round Andy's waist. It was fantastic.

It was during a hospital appointment to check a lump that had developed in my left breast in July 1986, that I discovered I was five weeks pregnant. I hadn't had the faintest idea, and felt surprised and excited when the doctor said that it was a possibility.

When I returned home that day, Andy was lying on the floor watching television. He jumped up and gave me a kiss as I sat down on the sofa.

'Would you like a brew?' he said, wanting to please.

'No thanks,' I said, 'but you might want a whisky with the news I have for you.'

'What do you mean?' he said, doing a double-take as he was walking out of the room.

'The doctor thinks I might be pregnant.'

His eyes became wider and his smile broader as he walked towards me.

'What do you mean, the doctor *thinks* you're pregnant?' he said. 'How do we find out for definite?'

'Listen, listen to me,' I said, smiling, 'If you don't keep quiet I can't tell you anything.'

Andy had barely let me say a word since I had told him the news — he seemed so excited and happy.

'What? What?' he asked.

I put my hand in my handbag and took out a small specimen bottle. 'I've got to pee in this tomorrow morning and take it to the hospital. Then we'll know for definite.'

As though it might be tempting fate to discuss the matter any further, we hardly mentioned the subject again that day, but we would sometimes look at each other, saying nothing, but those looks spoke volumes. I could tell Andy was wonderfully excited and I also hoped in my heart that I was pregnant.

The following morning, Andy was up early and off to the hospital with my specimen before going to camp. He had been told that we could phone at 2.00pm, and so Andy decided to come home for lunch so that he could be with me when I received the news.

I phoned at 2.00pm and spoke to a woman in the hospital laboratory.

'Daddy!' I shouted as I put down the phone.

'Yaaaarrrrroooo!' came the yell of delight from the lounge as he rushed to kiss me. He hugged and kissed me and made me sit on the sofa and offered me a cup of tea. Minutes later, the news seemed to have really sunk in when Andy looked at me, somewhat concerned: 'So, we're having a baby, then?'

'I think you could say that,' I replied.

He knelt on the floor, lifted up my shirt and put his hand on my stomach. 'Ssshh,' he said, 'I want to see if I can feel anything.'

'You won't feel anything for another three months,' I told him, and he seemed a little disappointed.

My parents, however, were somewhat taken aback when I broke the news, as they told me there had never before been a member of the family born out of wedlock.

During the telephone conversation, my father asked,

'Well, when's the wedding, then?'

I wasn't sure how to answer that, because Andy had asked me not to tell my parents about his previous marriages and I had gone along with it. Feeling so happy and excited about the prospect of having a baby, the one subject I didn't want to discuss was Andy's marriages and his current plans to divorce for the second time, especially as he was only 26!

'We're not marrying just because of the baby,' I said, somewhat guardedly, and I could sense my parents' disappointment.

But Andy and I, of course, *did* have a problem, as he wasn't yet divorced from Debbie and I had no idea which stage their divorce had reached. Whenever I broached the subject, Andy was reluctant to tell me anything about it. He would say that it was none of my business and that he would sort out the matter himself. I had known for months that I had to accept his point of view, but now I was pregnant with his baby I realised that one day I would want to marry him, not for convention's sake, but for the sake of my unborn child.

I waited anxiously for the occasion when Andy would talk about his divorce in the hope that one day we might discuss the subject of marriage. Whenever I raised the matter, no matter however tentatively, Andy would nearly always respond in the same way. 'It's getting sorted,' is all he would say and, as each week passed, my tummy became larger, and the more I feared that I would find myself an unmarried mum with no prospect of ever having a wedding.

Most of the time I would tell myself that I was

being stupid, because Andy was kind, attentive and understanding.

When he sensed my insecurity, he would tell me, 'Listen, Frances, you know how much I love my work, you know how much I love the Regiment, but they mean nothing compared to the way I love you.'

Hearing those words always gave me a feeling of warmth and tenderness towards Andy, and I would cease worrying about getting married ... for a while. I was fortunate that Andy remained at Hereford throughout most of my pregnancy, on what the SAS call 'team build-up'. This involves an SAS Squadron on exercises, practising their techniques as a team, such as staging mock attacks on aircraft, trains or buildings in which armed terrorists would be holding hostages.

The SAS has a fearsome and brilliant record of handling such incidents, and the Squadron on team build-up remains on stand-by for any such emergency. One SAS Squadron is always training at Hereford, ready to answer any emergency at a moment's notice.

The Squadron on team build-up is divided into two units, red and blue, which is an assault group and a sniper unit. Andy always loved being a member of the assault group because they are the ones who leap from helicopters, break into buildings and storm into hostile environments, throwing grenades and firing their Heckler & Koch weapons.

Andy never liked being in the sniper unit because he found the work boring. 'I much prefer the destructive action,' Andy would tell me, though he accepted that it was more dangerous.

Most emergencies in which SAS troops are involved occur outside Britain, when a foreign government will ask the British Government if the SAS can actively participate in a volatile situation, which might involve hostages, kidnaps or even, occasionally, taking out a well-entrenched unit of drug smugglers. It is most unusual for the British Cabinet not to give permission for such missions.

Nearly all such occasions, which the blokes call 'trips', are never made public but, within a matter of days, most of the wives at Hereford know precisely to which country the men have been sent, the reason for their trip and what they are doing. The husbands hate the fact that their wives know almost every detail.

On rare occasions, the wives know of forthcoming trips before their husbands. And that sometimes causes ructions within marriages, because wives aren't 'officially' meant to know where their husbands are working or what they are doing.

Quite often, wives who are meant to know nothing of their husbands' secret whereabouts, will receive postcards from the place when the mission is over. And they will usually be the ones checking the Barclaycards with details of their husbands' expenditure in the particular country they have been visiting.

Sometimes, wives hear of SAS missions from their husbands when they're asleep. One wife woke to hear her husband muttering a name over and over again. The following morning, before kissing her goodbye, the Sergeant told her, 'Sorry, I can't tell you where I am going, it's strictly hush-hush.'

'I know exactly where you're going,' she said.

'No you don't,' he said, 'this one's really secret.'

She immediately repeated the code word to him.

'Who told you?' he said angrily. 'How the hell did you find out? Only a dozen people are meant to know that. Tell me, go on, tell me where the hell you found out.'

'*You* told me,' she said.

'That's a bloody lie,' he said, 'I did *not* tell you.'

'Yes, you did,' she said, 'last night when you were asleep. You were talking in your sleep.'

'Shit!' he said. 'For God's sake, don't repeat it to a bloody soul, or you'll get me binned.'

And without another word he walked off down the path, not even bothering to look back as he did before most trips.

Two days later the story caused some amusement when the wife told the other wives about it during one of their coffee mornings.

Many husbands will return with a T-shirt for their wives with the name of the country or city they have just visited emblazoned on the chest. Most will tell their wives, 'I bought you this as a memento, but don't wear it around town, will you?'

There is also a most annoying aspect to the 'build-up' period, because the men have to carry the dreaded bleeper around with them. They are under the strictest orders to take the damn thing with them everywhere, and no excuses are permitted if they do not reply immediately to a call. Usually, a soldier who does not answer the call faces a fine. The teams alternate between having one month on a three-hour call-out, and the next on a 30-minute call-out.

Understandably, the wives find the bleeper an absolute pain, a nightmare, because the family cannot go off for a holiday, a weekend or even a night away from Hereford. And, of course, the bleepers have to be switched on 24 hours a day.

One night, Andy's bleeper went off shortly after we began making love.

'Don't answer it,' I pleaded.

'You know I must,' he said, 'I'm on a 30-minute call.' And as he had left the machine on the dressing-table, he went and checked.

'Bloody false alarm,' he said.

I couldn't resist making a point. 'Serves you right,' I told him, 'I told you not to answer it right away.'

Many SAS wives, though, hated team build-ups for another reason. They rather liked their husbands dashing off on exercises or missions in far-flung places because they simply enjoyed the break. They didn't like having to be perfect housewives, day in, day out, they didn't enjoy their lives becoming humdrum, and they missed the freedom.

By far and away the two favourite topics of conversation among most SAS wives was affairs and rumours of affairs and, of course, sex. Whenever a number of wives got together — at work, over coffee or while enjoying a drink — the topic of sex would surface almost immediately. Sex seemed to dominate our lives to a far greater degree than I would ever have imagined.

Those wives who had been married for some time would give advice to the younger, recently married women. They would tell them how to keep their man interested and how to keep him sexually attracted to them and to no one else.

They would advise the 'novices' to make sure their underwear was both new and sexy for the day their husbands arrived home. They would advise them to make sure their hair was looking good, the make-up near-perfect, and that they should appear as keen as ever for a great night and day of sex.

Most would recount the times their returning heroes would want sex the moment they had shut the front door, if not before. They would be told that most would be lucky to have the first bonk in bed because it would probably take place in the hall or living-room.

Those with children were advised to make sure they had arranged babysitters at whatever time of the day or night their men were expected home. 'If you don't,' they were told, 'you will regret it because your man will want them out of the way.'

They would sometimes add, 'And if you don't get it straight away, you will probably find yourselves fed up and irritable.'

Many wives would sit around trying to think of new ways of exciting their husbands on their return from overseas. All had thought of driving to Brize Norton to welcome their man dressed in stockings, suspenders and covered only by a mac. But I only ever heard of one wife who had actually tried it — it was a disaster.

Sarah, a young, attractive wife who had been a nurse before marrying into the SAS, told us what happened: 'I had read about it, seen it done in a film and the idea seemed sexy and attractive. I suppose I did it for a dare really, to prove to myself that I could do something wild and unpredictable.

'For a start, it was pouring with rain so my hair and make-up looked terrible. As I stood there waiting for them to come through the double doors, I felt like a drowned rat. And I felt embarrassed. All the other wives were looking at me and I could tell they knew that I was starkers underneath. When Jim arrived, he came up to me and kissed me on the forehead.

' "What the fuck do you think you're doing showing me up in front of my mates?" were his first words. "Everyone here knows you've got fuck-all on underneath. You're making me look a right plonker." And with that he grabbed his kit and marched off in front of me as though he didn't want anyone to know we were together. We drove back to Hereford almost in silence and I tried to cover myself up as much as possible.'

Sarah continued, 'It would be 48 hours before he forgave me, and then the cheeky bastard insisted on screwing me with nothing on except the fucking mac!'

The 'older' wives would also warn others not to become upset if their husbands did not come straight home, but preferred to have a few beers with their mates in Hereford. They were told not to take it personally but to understand that on some occasions, some men needed to take time to adjust to being back home.

Personally, I disagreed with that and argued the point whenever that subject came up. I don't think Andy ever did that to me, but he may have done. I doubted it because of the way he behaved when he did arrive home

— at those times, ice-cold showers wouldn't have stopped him.

Sometimes the advice wives picked up from one another ended in disaster and acrimony. One wife, called Kim, a well-built woman in her 30s, who told her friends that she had never had a bonk in the shower, decided to surprise her husband when he returned home. She led him upstairs and when she walked into the bathroom and started to undress he became deeply suspicious of his wife's unusual behaviour and accused her of having an affair with someone while he was overseas. He became so convinced of her adultery that he stormed out of the house, became roaring drunk in Hereford and had to be brought home in a taxi. The following morning he could remember nothing of their row or the attempted seduction. The wife told how she never tried the experiment again and he never mentioned the incident.

Many of the wives loved to have sex with their men dressed in their camouflage fatigues. I thought I was in the minority when, during one discussion, I happened to broach the subject. I was taken aback when most of the women laughed, and nearly all seemed to understand and share my enthusiasm.

'Yes, lovely, a real turn-on' was the general consensus. And everyone laughed when one very attractive young wife said, 'He looks much sexier in his fatigues than when he's naked. As far as I'm concerned, I wish he would keep his uniform on every time.'

Some of us wondered whether it was the sight of the uniforms that had attracted us to our husbands in the first place, and whether it was the constant sight of men in uniforms that kept us sexually interested.

During the same discussion, another wife said, 'I don't know about you girls, but I find their guns a great turn-on, too.'

'What do you mean?' three voices responded in unison.

'That's enough', she said, shyly, 'I've said enough already; I am saying nothing more.'

Some minutes later, she piped up: 'You should try it, you really should, you don't know how sexy a gun can be. It's better than the real thing.'

There were, of course, other more outrageous sexual antics which one or two of the SAS wives admitted to but, at that time, some seemed a little far-fetched.

Susan, who had been married for seven long years, and whose husband had become uninterested in the sexual side of their marriage, told a group of four of us during a girls night out at The Booth, a Hereford pub favoured by the Regiment and their partners, that she had tried everything to seduce him, but to no avail.

She would always refer to him as her 'old man', and feared that if he was not having nookey with her at home he must be meeting some floosie in Hereford. 'I became so desperate,' she said, 'that I started reading porno books in the hope of finding an idea that would do the trick. Eventually I found something which we had never tried. 'That night I put a chair in the middle of the bedroom and asked him to go along with my plan. After some persuasion, he agreed that he would do everything I asked without complaint. I tied him to the chair, placed plastic handcuffs around his wrists and taped his eyes.

Then I put on some loud music, stripped naked and began kissing him. 'Every few minutes I would give him a nip of whisky, sometimes taking a gulp myself and then squirting it into his mouth. It worked brilliantly. In no time I was sitting astride him.'

Then she stopped talking, but we kept asking her to continue, to tell us what happened next.

'If you really want to know, I'll tell you', she said, 'but only if you all keep quiet. The whole pub's listening in.'

We all kept quiet and Sue continued. 'There was only one problem. He became so turned on doing that he would insist we did it every night. Not only did I get fed up of doing all the work but it was bloody cold in winter. So now we're back to doing nothing again.'

We looked at each other and I was convinced that we were all having similar thoughts — that we might try the same experiment some time. There would be other kinky ideas the wives loved discussing and talking about, but nothing else that I found particularly outrageous.

Years later, however, I would discover my own needs and desires, the dark side of my sexuality.

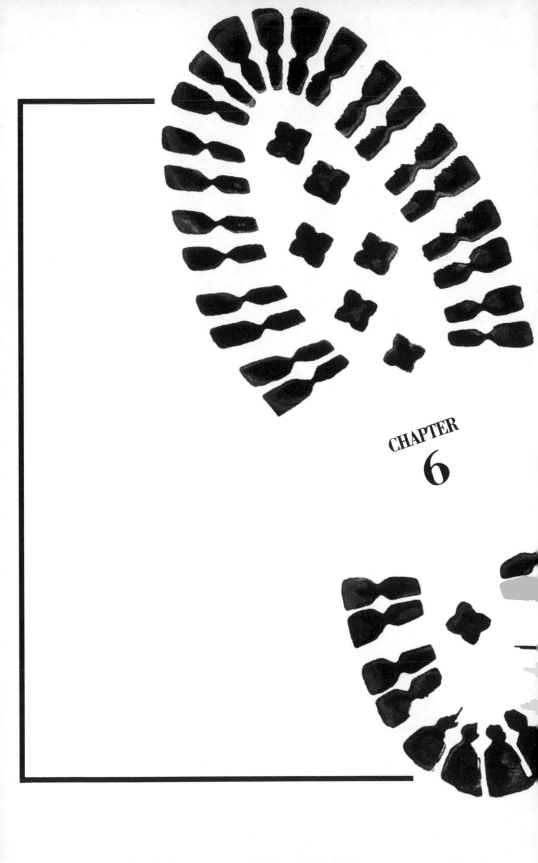

CHAPTER
6

> '**SAS philosophy includes the unrelenting pursuit of excellence and maintaining the highest standards of discipline.**'

COLONEL DAVID STIRLING

MY BELOVED JOANNA WAS BORN AT 5.30 on the afternoon of Monday, February 23 1987, in the maternity wing of Hereford County Hospital. She weighed 6lb 14oz, and had virtually no hair.

Andy was due to leave Hereford for a seven-week tour of duty, practising team drill in Nepal. We had both wanted Andy to be present at the birth.

He would say, 'I want to be there through every minute of this baby's birth. I want to hold your hand; I want us to be the first to hold our baby together. Nothing, nothing is more important than this child.'

Andy had been brilliant throughout the entire pregnancy. He would get up early every morning before going to work to ensure that he had time to bring my toast and mug of tea to me as I lay in bed. He would come home at lunchtime and make me something light, like chicken soup and hot bread.

For the first seven months of the pregnancy I was not at all well, suffering from chronic anaemia and spending most of the time in bed. He would come home at night and make dinner for us, anything I asked for, because he knew I had trouble eating and, more importantly, keeping down any food at all.

In my 27th week I was hospitalised for five days and they thought I would lose the baby. Andy was away on an exercise near Hereford at the time I was taken into hospital. I only had time to leave him a brief note on the kitchen table, telling him not to worry.

At 10.00pm one night I heard a commotion outside the ward and suddenly I saw a soldier in fatigues stride into the room. He looked at though he had just come straight from the Brecon Beacons, unshaven, unwashed and his fatigues covered in dirt. Although the ward was full of army wives all expecting babies, I knew instantly it was Andy. He looked concerned and physically shattered, as though he hadn't slept for a week.

'Are you sure you and the baby are going to be OK?' he kept asking, and I reassured him three or four times before it sunk in and he began to relax.

I happened to mention that the hospital nighties weren't very comfortable, and the following day he returned to see me having bought two very pretty lacy nighties. I loved him for that.

Later, the doctors were worried that my blood count was dangerously low and my brother, Gary, happily agreed to be on stand-by because they feared that after giving birth I would probably need an instant blood transfusion. In the event, however, everything was fine.

On 20 February Andy took me to hospital for a check-up and he then asked the doctor if he would consider inducing the baby because he was going overseas for several weeks and he desperately wanted to be with me when the baby was born. The doctor told him that he didn't like the idea of inducing a baby unless it was absolutely necessary, but they would keep me in to see how things went.

We had planned this baby's arrival down to the last detail, and we both wanted Andy to be present. He could see that I was becoming worried that I would be left on my own when the baby arrived, and he believed I would become distraught unless he was present.

When he returned home each night he would sleep, fully dressed, on the sofa by the phone in case he was called to the hospital.

It became a race against time. I tried my damndest to make the baby come quickly so that Andy could be present at the birth. The nurses gave me all the usual tips, telling me to have a really hot bath, take cod liver oil, and one or two jokingly suggested that I drink a bottle of gin!

Seven hours before he was due to leave Hereford for Nepal, the hospital rang to tell Andy that I had gone into labour and suggested he come to see me in a couple of hours. Within 15 minutes he was by my side.

Thirty minutes before Andy had to leave the hospital to ensure he did not miss the flight I had become distraught, as I was convinced that he would not be there for our baby's birth. They gave me pethedine and I calmed down. As the minutes passed, I realised Andy was about to leave me because the tears were welling in his eyes and I fought to give birth as quickly as possible.

But it was not to be.

'I'm sorry, Andy, I'm so sorry,' I sobbed. 'I can't make it. I've let you down. I so wanted to make it before you had to leave.'

'Sshh,' Andy said, 'don't fret; you've been wonderful. Now calm down; you need all your energy to bring this little one of ours into the world.'

He kissed me, squeezed my hand, and was gone.

He phoned six times as he waited for his flight at Heathrow that evening, but there was nothing to report. He told me later that he made his final call seconds before handing over his boarding card at the departure gate.

My mother answered his final call, and was able to tell him that two minutes earlier I had given birth to a baby girl and that Joanna and I were fine and well. I was so happy that we had produced a girl because I knew that would make Andy so happy. He would tell me that he and the lads celebrated with champagne for most of the flight.

Ten days later I took baby Jo home. She was fine. My mother had taken photographs of the birth and I sent these, along with the pictures of Jo at home, to Andy in Nepal. He loved them and wrote saying how he was hating the trip and was longing to return home to hold 'his' baby.

But during that exercise Andy became seriously ill, suffering from amoebic dysentry, but he never wrote to tell me, fearing that I would worry.

I was determined to try and look at my best for Andy's homecoming. Seven weeks after the birth I still felt frumpy, unattractive and overweight, even though I was still wearing size 10 clothes. My mother bought me a pale blue sweater and navy-blue trousers, but I still believed I wasn't looking very good.

I was expecting to see Andy bounding up the path to see Joanna and me. All that night I felt nervous and excited. When I heard a car pull up outside at about 8.00am, I rushed to the bedroom window to see if it was Andy. I caught my breath in astonishment as I saw a man I recognised as Andy being helped from the car. He seemed hardly able to walk up the path unaided and I all but flew down the stairs to see what had happened.

'What's the matter?' I asked him. 'Are you alright?'

'Yes, I'm fine,' he said trying to smile, but I could see he was forcing himself for his eyes betrayed him. He looked exhausted and empty and I had never seen Andy other than fit, healthy and bursting with vitality.

'Let me look at her, let me look at her,' he said, but he felt so weak that he didn't want to risk holding her himself. It was only when he sat down in a chair that he asked to hold her and I found myself looking at him, wondering what on earth had happened and knowing I must wait and let him tell me.

Eventually he told me that he had been infected by some badly cooked meat and the dysentry had hit him particularly hard. He was hospitalised along with others of the Troop who had also become infected, and had lost more than two stone in weight.

Johnny Two-Combs also fell ill, seriously ill, and doctors feared he had contracted typhoid. Fortunately, they discovered later that he was only suffering from a ruptured appendix. He would recover. Johnny told me later that the doctors had informed him that he had nearly died in the Nepalese hospital and thought that he would never make it back home.

I knew I would have to care for Andy, to try and help him recover. He showed great courage throughout his rehabilitation as he was suffering great pain around his intestines. And yet he would try to fob it off, telling me he was fine.

I would get up early and take his breakfast to the bedroom so he could rest, but he resented being treated like an invalid. On one occasion, I heard him thumping the walls in the bathroom. I ran upstairs to see what was happening and I saw him punching the walls with his fists as though trying to injure himself.

'What's the matter?' I cried out. 'What are you doing to yourself?'

'It's the only way I know to transfer the pain,' he said. 'My guts are giving me hell and the pain seems to go if I inflict pain into my hands by smashing the walls.'

'Are you sure?' I asked rather sceptically, 'I've never heard doctors recommending that as a way to ease pain.'

'I don't care a fuck what the doctors think,' he told me. 'I know it works for me and a lot of my mates.'

After a few more violent punches, he turned and braced himself. 'See,' he said, 'now I feel much better; the pain in my guts has disappeared.'

But we both knew the pain would return later. And it did.

After only a short leave Andy returned to work, getting up early and going to camp as usual. I would ask him, time and again, if he felt well enough for work, because I could see the pain in his eyes and that his strength had not fully returned. But he never wanted to talk about it, as though admitting to the pain and tiredness made him appear weak and not tough enough to be a member of the SAS.

'I'm fine,' he would tell me, 'I'm A-OK. Just leave me alone, will you, and let me be.'

I would talk to Hayley, an SAS wife who had been married for six years and had lived in Hereford throughout that time. I believe that Hayley knew more about the men than they did themselves.

I told her that I was worried about Andy, that I was convinced he was ill, but that he pretended everything was fine.

'You will never get them to admit they are ill,' she told me, 'they try to shake it off. They hate to admit that they are ever ill or injured. And they won't accept pain. They believe they can overcome pain by disregarding it. Sometimes it works, but I don't know how.'

She would explain to me in some detail how she believed their bravado was necessary because it inured them against wounds and injuries when on active service missions.

'They are taught not to feel pain,' she told me. 'They are made to forget injuries and pay no attention to them until the mission is completed. In that way, they are never a liability to one another. It's a brilliant psychological tactic by the SAS, ensuring that their soldiers can keep going under the most extraordinarily adverse conditions, and can sometimes override great physical pain.'

Hayley told me stories of SAS men on missions who had continued fighting when they had a foot blown off by a land mine; of a soldier who discovered he had been hit six times in the legs by automatic fire but kept running until he collapsed through loss of blood; of a third SAS man who hadn't noticed that his elbow had been totally shattered by gunfire until he realised he couldn't hold his rifle.

'They don't put it down to bravery or courage,' Hayley told me, 'they put it down to their rigorous training and their 'never-say-die' attitude to every situation. You must understand that these men believe they are indestructible, and behave as if they are while there is still breath in their bodies. That's what the training is all about and it works wonders.'

She explained that their training ensures that an SAS man is taught to focus on a particular objective, whether it is lying low in the banks of a *wadi* in the Middle East for days, hiding in swamps up to their necks in water for hours at a time, or taking out an armed unit holed up in a heavily defended position. Told to carry out an order, they will do so against the most extraordinary odds and with absolute obedience. 'That's what makes the SAS such a brilliant fighting force,' she said.

It would take Andy nearly 12 months to recover totally, to become transformed back to the man I had known before his trip to Nepal.

But it took Andy a while to adjust to having a baby around the house. Within a couple of weeks, however, he surprised me by the attention and love he gave Jo. He would carry her everywhere, wanting to hold her and to be seen with his baby out shopping. He adored her and, understandably, he wanted everyone else to love her, too. And they did.

He would insist on pushing her in the pram, wanting everyone to stop and look at her. He would chat to her non-stop, about everything and about nothing. He would talk about the weather, the shopping, his clothes and even about politics and the state of the world!

To my great surprise, he also took Jo into camp with him to show her off to everyone who hadn't yet seen her around Hereford. He adored her.

He was also concerned that she didn't sleep longer than 20 minutes at a time. At first, he loved the idea of picking her up when she awoke, holding her in bed at night, and he became a dab hand at changing her nappy.

But when Jo continued to wake each hour, every hour, the attraction of getting up to her six or seven times a night began to wear off. 'Does every baby work like this?' he asked me once.

When I explained that all babies were different, and

that many slept peacefully throughout the night, he was not so pleased. 'Typical,' he replied, 'trust us to have the wake-up type.'

We would try everything to get Joanna to sleep, driving miles every night of the week in the hope that she would drop off. She would sleep almost as soon as we set off in the car, but the moment we came home and stopped she would wake up and want to play. I was surprised how patient Andy was with Jo, because he was tired and unwell during those first few months and he needed his sleep. Perhaps it was the SAS training, but he proved formidable in showing patience and gentleness with Jo when he must have been feeling exhausted.

A few weeks after Andy returned from Nepal, we moved to rented accommodation while the house we had bought was being completed by the builders. Our rented home on the outskirts of Hereford was a three-bedroom, semi-detached house giving us more space.

Andy had told me that he had been led to believe that his divorce from Debbie would be finalised in August of that year and we had, from time to time, discussed the idea that we would marry one day. Deep down I wanted to marry Andy, and I was looking forward to being known as Mrs Frances McNab. I also wanted Jo to have married parents.

There was another important point. If a woman is not legally married to an SAS man she is not accepted as part of the big SAS family. Even if a woman has a baby and the couple live together as man and wife for a number of years, a girlfriend is never treated by the

Regiment with the same courtesy and respect that a wife earns simply by courtesy of the legally binding marriage certificate.

Many girlfriends living with SAS soldiers, including me, were made to feel like second-class citizens, not to be trusted to the same extent, and never provided with the same information that all wives are given when their husbands are away on a mission or training exercise.

Furthermore, if a girlfriend, or common-law wife, approaches an SAS officer with any complaints, she is heard sympathetically and the officer generally appears to take note. In reality, however, every girlfriend or ex-wife knows the SAS does not want to know about girlfriends or ex-wives who might, heaven forbid, come between the soldier and the Regiment. The officers show concern for the soldiers in their Squadron and the Regiment, and they will care for wives, but girlfriends and ex-wives are treated with little or no concern.

A number of ex-wives were actively encouraged to leave Hereford for fear of possible future embarrassment when their ex-husband begins a new relationship.

And the barriers become even more impregnable if an ex-wife wishes to complain about the behaviour of her former husband, or the fact that no maintenance has been paid to the children of a former marriage. Once again, the SAS Families' Officer will listen sympathetically but most ex-wives report that nothing ever comes of a complaint because the SAS will always, seemingly, take the side of their soldiers, even when the evidence is overwhelmingly against them.

*   *   *

By the summer of 1987, I decided that the time had come to see whether Andy was serious when he told me that he wanted us to marry as soon as his divorce came through. I needed to know what future both Jo and I had with Andy, as I didn't want us to remain on the periphery of SAS life in Hereford.

One summer's day while out shopping with Jo, I saw a sweet little engagement ring in a jeweller's shop which was frequently used by men from the Regiment. The jeweller would give them a discount, like many of the shops around Hereford.

'Shall we tell Daddy what we saw today, darling?' I said to Jo that evening, knowing that Andy was listening to our baby-talk.

'What was that?' he asked.

'We saw this little solitaire diamond ring, which was really sweet and very inexpensive,' I babbled.

'And how much was this ring?' Andy enquired.

'Just £100,' I said, 'and, if you would care to know, it fitted my finger to perfection, didn't it Jo?'

'I see,' said Andy and the subject was dropped.

I wondered if I had made a mistake in bringing up the subject because Andy said nothing. However, some time later he raced upstairs saying his bleeper had gone off, and he came down saying he had to return to camp immediately. He would be back for dinner.

I was feeling somewhat dejected that evening as I cooked a casserole for dinner, knowing that Andy might return any time between 7.00pm and midnight. For once, Jo had fallen asleep after her bath and I hoped for a few hours peace.

Andy returned home earlier than I expected and when I walked into the living-room I saw a lovely bunch of roses on the dining-room table. Next to them was a card and a little purple box, which I felt convinced was my ring.

Before I realised what was happening, I felt Andy behind me putting his arms around my waist and kissing the nape of my neck.

'Go on,' he said, 'open it.'

I felt so happy as I opened the box and saw the sweet, delicate diamond I had seen that morning. The card simply read, 'How about it then? Love always, Andy.'

I asked him to get on one knee and put the ring on my finger, and although he looked embarrassed he went through with the little ceremony. I loved him for buying me the ring and proposing to me in his inimitable manner. I also loved him more for being a sport and going through with his declaration of love on one knee. Now I had the commitment I wanted and I felt a happier, more relaxed woman.

Later that night as we lay together in bed, Andy wanted to discuss when we would be married. I had been happy simply having the commitment of an engagement ring, but he seemed keen to sort out our future life together.

He knew that within the next six months he would be sent to Northern Ireland on detachment for a long, two-year stint working with the 'Det', a highly secretive intelligence gathering unit working undercover. He told me that the SAS has asked for volunteers but no one had come forward, so it was decided that two men from each Squadron would be detailed. Andy and his pal Eno were selected. They had no wish to go but were given no option by the Commanding Officer. In no uncertain terms they were told that if they didn't go to Northern Ireland, they would be kicked out of the Regiment. They agreed to go.

The next day, Andy came home and offered me three dates for our wedding. I spoke to my parents, phoned the Hereford Registry Office and organised a date in autumn 1987.

One weekend in August we went to see his parents in Kent, because Andy wanted to tell them of our forthcoming marriage. His mother, a charming, white-haired woman in her 50s, and his father, a London taxi driver, seemed thrilled at the news and happy that we were marrying for Jo's sake.

Before we left, however, his mother made a comment which Andy would soon forget. She took him to one side and told him, 'I hope that this is your last marriage, Andy, because three daughters-in-law are more than enough for any mother.' Andy told me this as we drove away.

'How did you reply?' I enquired.

'I said nothing,' he said honestly. 'I just laughed.'

A couple of weeks before our wedding, we were able to move into our brand-new three-bedroom, semi-detached house in a quiet cul-de-sac on the outskirts of

Hereford. We would only live there for five months before selling the place and making a remarkable £17,000 profit!

The day before the wedding, Andy looked out of the window to see that the heavens had opened and the rain was bucketing down. We listened to the forecast which predicted more heavy rain for the next 48 hours. We looked at each other in disappointment, but knew that the rain didn't really matter because our reception was booked for the following day in Gosport, Hampshire, where my parents lived.

'Did you book a photographer?' Andy asked, checking the list of everything that had to be done for the great day.

'Yes,' I replied.

'Well,' he said, 'with this piss-awful rain I think it's a waste of money having a photographer for the wedding. You can cancel him and I'll ask my brother to take the snaps. Remember, he is a first-class photographer. And on Saturday lots of people will take photos at the reception.'

His brother did take the photographs, loads of them, but we would never see a single one because, quite by accident, the photos were lost.

The morning of the wedding I drove down to the bridal shop in Hereford, keen to pick up my heavily-embroidered, off-white fitted suit with long sleeves. The jacket looked wonderful. Then I went to put on the matching knee-length skirt and I could not even get it above my thighs. In desperation I looked for a zip or buttons that had not been unfastened but the zip was already undone and there were no buttons!

'Excuse me,' I called out to the assistant, 'I think you must have given me the wrong skirt; I can't even get it above my thighs.'

'No, love,' she said, 'I know it's the right one because it's the only one we have.' And she walked off.

I left the fitting room and asked the assistant what I should do as I was getting married in six hours' time. She advised me to search Hereford to try and find a matching off-white skirt. I was becoming distressed and rather upset. In my heart, I had always wanted to marry in a lovely white dress in a beautiful church with the organ playing the Wedding March; now I was planning to marry in a Registry Office in an off-white jacket and skirt which didn't even match!

I walked around Hereford with my mother, but we could find nothing to match the jacket. When we finally returned to the shop, the manageress had arrived and she offered me the choice of any new wedding gown for the price of a rented one. I quite liked the one we selected, but I wasn't unhappy that I had to hand it back afterwards.

When we returned home, Andy was still caring for Jo, playing with her on the rug having fed her and changed her nappy. He didn't seem to mind that my suit hadn't fitted or that I had to rent a wedding dress. 'It doesn't matter darling,' is all he said, trying to cheer me up, 'I wouldn't mind if you were dressed in jeans for our wedding, because I just want to be with you.'

He was very sweet but he simply didn't seem to understand that a girl likes to have everything 'just perfect' for her wedding day, and not be forced into having to rush around looking for something to wear.

Unfortunately, the weather forecast was accurate. It rained heavily throughout the day and nearly everyone was soaked at one time or another. I wasn't in the best of moods and felt as though we were in a doctor's waiting room as we waited for our turn in the queue. Andy, too, seemed edgy and nervous, and I wondered what was going through his mind.

As a joke, I whispered to Andy, 'You're lucky, darling, you must know the words off by heart by now.'

He laughed and gave me a kiss. 'But I'm still nervous,' he added.

After dinner at The Starting Gate, a restaurant in Hereford, we drove in a mini-bus to Gosport for the reception the following day. Everyone was so exhausted by the time we arrived at my parents' house that everyone went straight to bed and both Andy and I were asleep before the marriage could be consummated.

The reception at my father's pub in Gosport was a great affair. The sun was shining, many of my old friends and most of my family, some of whom I hadn't seen for years, all enjoyed a wonderful day. Andy surprised everyone with the bridegroom's speech because people expected an amusing, long, jokey, knock-about address, because they knew Andy's talkative nature. In the event he only said a dozen words and asked his Best Man, Dave, to speak instead!

The champagne never stopped flowing and Andy had such a wonderful time that he all but passed out on the disco floor at 8.00pm. I had booked the bridal suite in the nearby Angelsea Hotel for our wedding night, but Andy suggested that I cancel it and take him home to sleep off the effects of the booze. It wasn't until we returned to our lovely home at Hereford on the Sunday night that we finally consummated our marriage!

I lay awake that night with something troubling me. I felt there was something missing in our relationship and that concerned me. It seemed we had become almost strangers to each other and that the very act of marrying had somehow disrupted the good relationship we had been enjoying. I told myself, over and over again, that my fears were unfounded and that all would be fine in the morning.

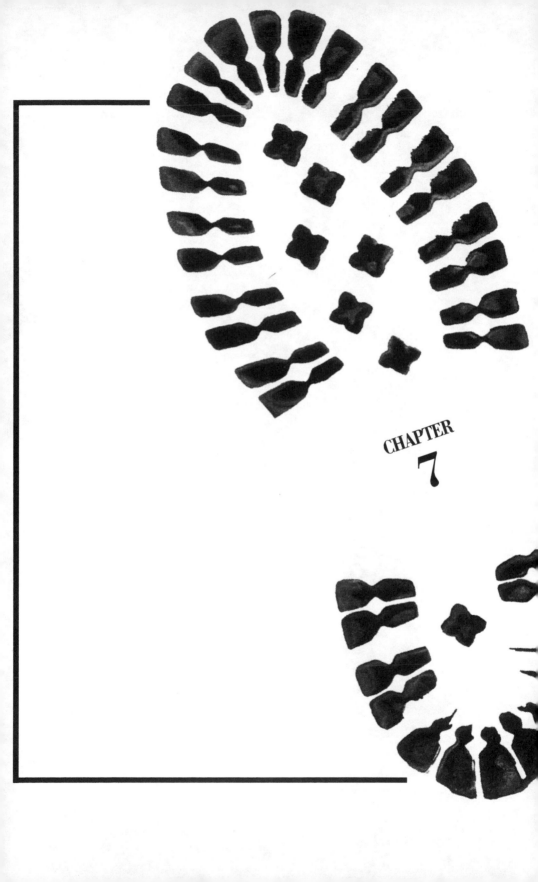

CHAPTER
7

'The SAS brooks no sense of class and, particularly, not among the wives.'

COLONEL DAVID STIRLING

DRIVING INTO STIRLING LINES, the home of the SAS, Britain's élite Regiment of troops, was, on most occasions, easier than walking into a children's playground. The security on the gates was so lax no one bothered to ask for a pass or seek a name or identification from total strangers!

When I first arrived at the camp, in the passenger seat of a Golf GTi in the middle of the 1980s, when the IRA had sworn vengeance against the SAS, we drove straight through the main gates which were guarded by one Ministry of Defence policeman who didn't appear to be carrying any type of weapon.

I felt rather nervous that first time I arrived at the barracks. I expected to be stopped, asked to leave the car, produce identification, state my reasons for visiting the base, name the person I wanted to see, and sign an entry log stating the date and time of my arrival, as well as the car's registration number.

I recalled the procedure whenever I visited my father's base at HMS Dolphin at Gosport when I was an innocent 14-year-old. I would be marched to the Guard Room by two guardsmen and would be asked to give my name and address and the reason for my visit to the base. It was, in fact, usually to take my father his sandwiches because he had left them at home. Even then I was not permitted to go further than the Guard Room. I waited while they telephoned my father and he would come to see me.

We drove slowly through the wide-open main gate and the police officer on duty stayed in his little brick built lodge and simply waved to us. We never stopped, never showed any pass but drove to the car park 200 yards distant, parked and walked into the heart of the camp.

As we drove past the officer, I said to my boyfriend driving the car, 'Is that it?'

'What do you mean?' he asked.

'Well, is there no security check, nothing here?'

'They don't bother too much,' he said. 'I think that guy recognised me.'

'But he didn't know *me*,' I said. 'He has never seen me before in his life.'

'Well,' he said, 'remember, this is the SAS. Someone might find it very easy to walk into this place but they would never walk out alive.'

'And what if the IRA decided to attack?'

'They wouldn't dare,' he said. 'Not one would survive.'

'But when we drove in, I could have been holding a gun to your side and there could have been a couple more terrorists in the back of the car.'

He laughed, 'It's not quite as open as it seems,' he said.

The entire base, situated opposite a council housing estate a mile from the centre of Hereford, would always appear to be open house for anyone wanting to visit, with or without permission. After I had lived in Hereford for a couple of years, however, security at the base was tightened and people going in and out had to produce passes. But many didn't bother to do so.

The perimeter fencing was simply a nine-foot-high, single-wire fence topped with barbed wire. When men from the Regiment couldn't be bothered walking the extra few hundred yards around to the main gate from the houses which backed on to the camp, they would simply climb the fence and drop into the base.

I was at a party at one of the houses one night when an SAS soldier told me he was leaving. It was raining and I told him he would get soaked walking back to his 'basha' (SAS slang for a room or shelter).

'Don't be silly,' he said, 'I'll nip over the fence. We always do. Saves time.'

And I watched, somewhat surprised, as he walked

out of the party, ran down the back garden of the house and jumped up and over the wire. I waited to see if any lights would come on or if he would trip an alarm. I saw and heard nothing.

Stirling Lines seemed to me to be the most casual military camp in Britain. When anyone walks through the gates it seems as if you are entering a college campus rather than a military establishment dedicated to efficiency, professionalism and security. On entering the camp, there is hardly ever a uniform to be seen — the men mostly walk around in casual clothing and, during the summer months, opt for shorts and T-shirts.

The fact that the men wear their hair any length, depending on what task they are doing at the time, gives the impression of a casual college base. The Clock Tower (a memorial on which the names of the SAS dead are written) is the only recognisable focal point suggesting a military camp.

No soldiers march around the camp — the men simply stroll around as though relaxing on holiday. No one is seen smartly saluting senior officers, because the troops simply acknowledge each other with a casual 'Hi'. No one stands to attention or attends drill because there is no such thing as 'square bashing' in the SAS, and there is no Sergeant-Major bellowing orders at the top of his voice, because all orders are delivered *sotto voce*, usually behind closed doors. And the men of the SAS never call their senior officers 'Sir' but always 'Boss', the same term that professional footballers use when talking to their coaches and managers.

And it is not only the men and their wives who find

it remarkably easy to enter the hallowed portals of the nation's crack fighting force. Single, unattached girls, as well as wives and ex-wives of SAS soldiers, seemed to be able to walk in and out of Stirling Lines without any fuss, trouble or question. They would enter through the back of the camp where all visitors were met by two SAS soldiers on sentry duty, dressed in camouflage fatigues, sporting their traditional sand-coloured berets and their pale blue belts. They carried sub-machine guns and I was told that the weapons were always loaded with live rounds.

The SAS sentries would stand behind a high, metal grille gate which would be opened by a switch inside the gate house close by. Wives, of course, would be issued with a pass, but there were often numbers of other girls who fancied a night out at The Paludrine club. Often the girls would take a taxi to the base and chat up the sentries who would usually let the girls in without much resistance. If girls were denied entry, then they would usually wait around for a few minutes and find an SAS soldier prepared to take them in as his guests.

It was noted by all the wives that any attractive, pretty girl would always be admitted without question but that less attractive visitors might have some trouble gaining access. Nurses were always encouraged to visit the club whenever they wanted and, occasionally, car-loads would arrive at once and would be given immediate access, without having to show any passes or undergo searches of their handbags or clothing for any concealed weapons.

One night I met a girl I knew from the chicken

factory where I worked, who wanted to visit The Paludrine with another friend. They had been refused access and were waiting for someone to take them in. I offered to help.

'Oh, thanks a lot,' the girl said. 'Do you want the money for a drink?'

'Of course not,' I said. 'Why would I want money for a drink?'

'Well, whenever we have difficulty getting into the club, the soldiers charge us for either a pint or two pints as a sort of entrance fee. It always works. One girl was so desperate she offered to give a soldier more than a kiss if he would get her in. He took her into the base and straight to his room.'

*　　　*　　　*

Over the past few years, the SAS has attracted a great deal of attention because of its high-profile successes around the world. Military and civil VIPs are regular visitors to SAS bases, and they are often invited to attend demonstrations to appreciate the Regiment's capabilities.

One of the principal attractions of Stirling Lines was the fabled Killing House, the 'CQB' building — close-quarter battle building — constructed specifically to enable the SAS to train in hostage rescue and covert entry using live ammunition. The Killing House was a single-storey building with a central corridor and different-sized rooms leading off either side. The rooms were constructed of portable partitions so they could be changed around, and piles of furniture were stacked in each room to act as barricades against 'attacking' SAS troops. Some rooms were constructed with bullet-proof glass walls with tiny portholes, where VIPs as well as army instructors could view the action. It is also from those vantage positions that instructors would video-tape the troops, showing them later where they went wrong and how they could improve techniques.

The troops did not mind showing off their skills in the Killing House to high-ranking VIPs (senior politicians, Chief Constables, and so on), but they resented having to repeat the exercises over and over again for teams of doctors, nurses, firemen and rugby teams!

The world heard of the day Princess Diana visited the Killing House with Prince Charles in 1986 and agreed to take part in an exercise where live ammunition would be used. At the end of the day, the royal couple agreed to act as hostages, waiting in the Killing House for the SAS to save them. During the operation, Diana and Charles were 'imprisoned' in a room into which 'flashbangs' were thrown. Flashbangs are very noisy grenades designed to disorientate the victims. One fool of a trooper threw one a little too carelessly, hitting Diana on the head and singeing her hair.

At the time, she was remarkably cool about the incident and there were many apologies. Days later, the newspapers showed her with a much shorter haircut, acclaiming a new fashion trend initiated by the Princess. It was nearly ten years later that the truth became known.

However, very few people heard of Diana's anger when she returned to the privacy of a room set aside for the royal couple. She looked in the mirror to inspect the damage and complained bitterly and angrily at the 'bloody fool' who had ruined her hair. But, at the time, no one heard that side of the royal 'tragedy'.

Prime Minister Margaret Thatcher visited Stirling Lines on a number of occasions and became one of their greatest fans. And the troops, knowing that the Prime Minister supported them so enthusiastically, were happy to put on any number of demonstrations for their favourite politician. It seemed as though there was all but a love affair between Thatcher and the Regiment.

When SAS troops are on team build-up or on a training course at Hereford, it seems they are unable to keep away from the camp for more than a few hours at a time. Many wives cannot understand why their men want to spend so much time in camp, when they could be at home with them and their children.

Most wives hear the same story over and over again. Their husbands complain bitterly of spending so much time away from their families, hating being parted from their children, their loved ones and always talking of jacking in the Army and returning to a normal, civilised life on the outside. But after the first few months of listening to that scratched record repeated *ad nauseam*, the wives realise only too well that the complaints are nothing but empty words.

The SAS becomes a drug to many of the young soldiers, especially during the first few years of being 'badged', passing the extraordinarily tough entrance procedure and being accepted into the unit. No sooner are they back from a training exercise, than they have to return to camp to be with their mates, hear the gossip and swap tales. Officially, they tell their wives that they are attending 'debriefing sessions'.

Moreover, the great majority of SAS wives say that their husbands go to the camp for several hours a day whether they are on or off duty, attending a course or officially on leave. The camp seems to act as a sort of powerful magnet.

The soldiers somehow need to know exactly what is going on at all times, fearful that they might not have heard of the latest mission, exercise or piece of gossip.

There is another reason why many married men spend so much time at the camp. Most of them keep at least one spare set of clothes at camp so that they can change to go out on the town or enjoy illicit affairs. Their wives have no idea they have clothes hidden in camp. They also keep what they describe as their 'slush funds' at camp, their secret bank or building society accounts which their wives know nothing about. That money is for their personal expenditure, either drinking nights with their mates or naughty nights with their mistresses. Some even have one or two secret credit cards and arrange to have the monthly statements sent to the camp's mail box.

Breakfast at the base is a must for every SAS soldier interested in the camp gossip for it is then that details of the secret activities are revealed, talked about in great detail and dissected. The conversation involves just two subjects — sex and booze.

Andy would return from some breakfasts discrediting those blokes who discussed their conquests, and then he would proceed to tell me a string of juicy stories in all their glory. Other wives would tell me the same, although every husband would maintain he was not in the least interested.

The men would boast of all types of conquests, making their sexual adventures sound like the Oympics. Some would happily lie about the girls they had bonked, always naming names and seemingly not caring a damn about the girls' reputations.

One night I went home with Jean and an SAS man called Sam, a well-built, athletic man in his 30s, and we stayed talking until 3.00am munching our way through a bowl of sweets and chocolates. We had a hilarious time swapping jokes, gossiping and drinking wine.

Two days later, Jean's boyfriend came into the house shouting and swearing at her, demanding to know why she had enjoyed an orgy with me and Sam. She was completely taken aback. The argument raged non-stop for hours and he refused to believe her denials. She told him over and over again exactly what had happened, but the fact that the three of us had spent three hours together in her house seemed to prove our guilt. He refused to believe that we had only talked, eaten sweets and had a drink.

Later she phoned me to tell me what had happened and I offered to go round and see her boy friend to tell him that the gossip was totally unfounded.

'I don't think it will have any effect,' she told me.

'But we did nothing, absolutely nothing, except eat sweets and talk,' I said, outraged on her behalf.

'I tried that,' Jean said, 'it was no good. He told me

that he believed Sam completely because he was in the SAS and he knew he would never tell him a lie.'

The allegation had such an impact on their relationship that within six months they had separated.

*   *   *

Occasionally, of course, fights would break out between the younger SAS soldiers, but these would be immediately stamped out by the Regiment. Everyone who joined the Regiment was warned that anyone caught fighting would risk being immediately RTU'd. Nevertheless, when worse for wear, the occasional fight would take place.

SAS officers understand that the troops under their command are all extremely fit, very committed and keen to prove their strength, athleticism and capabilities. They are also quick to react to any criticism and even quicker to use their fists. The senior officers also realise that there is tremendous rivalry between the four Squadrons which make up 22 SAS.

One Saturday night, a fight broke out at The Booth in Hereford over a beer-drinking contest between two blokes from different Squadrons. I was having a quiet drink with a group of SAS men and wives and we heard some shouting going on. Suddenly the whole bar seemed to be heaving and when I stood up I could see fists flying. A group of young men, some I recognised as SAS members, were throwing themselves into the mêlée and the shouting reached a crescendo. Most of the blokes seemed to be trying to stop the others from fighting —

they were all aware of the disciplinary measures if the police were called.

After a few minutes, the four men punching and fighting each other were dragged away by their mates. We learned later that the fight broke out when one soldier accused another of cheating in a beer-drinking contest.

On that occasion everyone avoided trouble but, from time to time, SAS men found fighting were brought before the CO, reprimanded and warned.

More interesting would be the fights that broke out between young women, although these were few and far between. One famous occasion became the talk of Hereford for weeks, where the girlfriend of a member of D Squadron was at the bar at The Paludrine with her boyfriend, when another girl came up to him and asked him to dance. The soldier had not been dancing for more than a minute when a fist flashed past his face and crashed into the jaw of his dancing partner, sending her sprawling to the floor. Women screamed and the girl staggered to her feet, helped by a couple of the soldiers. She walked away, not wishing to risk the wrath of the soldier's girlfriend again.

Apparently, it transpired that the girl saw the other young woman caressing her boyfriend's buttocks, so she decided to act. Understandably, the young SAS soldier became the focus of attention for some time, and he revelled in his notoriety. Not many SAS men had women fighting over them, although they all loved being the centre of attention.

On another occasion, a fight broke out in the ladies'

loo and two girls were seen grabbing each other by the hair and trying to hit and scratch each other, screaming as they fought. Most of the women present left them to it and quickly left the room. No one ever knew the reason for that fight.

*   *   *

The SAS men would eat in the Sergeants' Mess and we would sometimes visit the mess for lunch, occasionally for dinner and, on special occasions, for breakfast. Everyone would eat at long tables and the chatter would never cease. I felt rather shy in the company of so many men all chomping away and being somewhat indiscreet in their conversations, and so I would find myself observing them and listening to everything they said.

I would also watch the wives and girlfriends on such occasions and realised that beneath the surface there was great sexual tension, with many of the wives seemingly more interested in men other than their husbands. At first I didn't notice what was happening, but the longer I stayed at Hereford and mixed with the SAS wives, the more I understood how fragile many relationships and marriages became in such short a time.

As a result of such meetings, I would wait to see how the couples behaved towards each other and how their relationships prospered. But, sadly, you would often hear later that a couple had separated or divorced. It would make me realise that I would need to work hard to keep my marriage happy and interesting and hope that Andy felt the same way.

And then there was the infamous 'Patch', the Stirling Lines married quarters where families of those attached to the Regiment lived, as well as a few whose husbands were badged members of the Regiment.

The Patch — consisting of mainly 1950s-style, flat-roofed terraced houses with two or three bedrooms, a living-room and dining-room — also included the Hereford NAAFI, a play school and a play area with swings and roundabouts.

On the surface, the Patch seemed a tranquil estate with the women going about their daily business and children playing in the streets. Behind the net curtains, however, the reputations of many who lived there were nowhere near as peaceful.

I was fortunate that I never had to live there, because I had been warned by a close girlfriend that living on the Patch could be dangerous and rather unpleasant.

Jane, an intelligent, down-to-earth woman in her late 20s with mousey hair, told me of her experiences of living on the Patch with her husband, a member of 264 Signals Squadron.

'The Patch wives became very cliquey. As soon as I arrived, I was visited by half-a-dozen of the young wives, ostensibly to welcome me and make me feel at home. I soon learned, however, that the wives were actually checking me out to see whether I measured up to their requirements. If I hadn't, I wouldn't be invited to any coffee mornings. I was later told that the first two or three wives who came to see me found me too stuck-up and thought I would never fit in. Finally, they accepted me, but within a few months I was screaming to escape from the area, as many of the women seemed absolute bitches.

'Many of them assumed their husbands' rank and expected the wives married to lower ranks to show the correct deference they believed they were due. Some would even expect junior wives to stand up and offer them their chairs when they walked into the room; others would expect to be heard on any subject and would demand their say before other lower-rank wives.

'This, of course, would lead to tremendous rivalry and jealousy and not a little bitchiness towards the older women.'

Jane told me of the day she had some new furniture delivered, just a dining-room table and six chairs. At the next coffee morning, she overheard two women talking about her new furniture, suggesting she had only bought six chairs because she wanted to show off to the neighbours that she threw dinner parties.

Those women who bought new furniture for their homes were often described as 'snobs', but those who could not afford new furniture and relied on property supplied by the Army were labelled 'slobs'. It was impossible to win.

Jane persuaded her husband that they had to leave the Patch because the back-biting was becoming intolerable. From the moment other wives heard she was moving away, they dropped her, never inviting her to any meetings and virtually ignoring her if they met her out shopping or in a pub.

During the late 1980s, with the price of housing rocketing every month, some SAS families decided to sell, take the profit and move on to the Patch. That would cause more problems because none of the wives married to attached personnel wanted anything at all to do with the badged wives whom they believed were a toffee-nosed bunch of young women, married only to SAS men for their bravado and prestige.

They would often spend coffee mornings trying to predict which SAS marriages would fail and how quickly. They believed for some reason that their marriages were made in heaven, that they would last for ever. Often their predictions were accurate, but many would also face disappointment as their own marriages would fail, too.

Jane was fortunate. Her marriage survived, and she believed one of the reasons was the fact that they escaped the bitchiness of the Patch. She thought mine would win through as well.

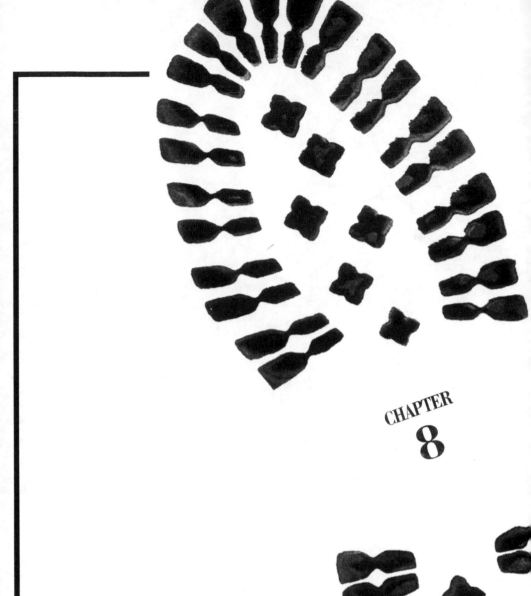

CHAPTER
8

'I don t think I have ever lived the sort of life which I could ask a woman to share.'

COLONEL DAVID STIRLING

IN LATE 1987, ANDY BEGAN HIS TWO-YEAR TOUR OF DUTY in Northern Ireland, not with the SAS, but as a member of a special intelligence gathering unit known as the 'Det' — the specialist military surveillance unit detached from their own Regiment.

Before going to Ireland, Andy and the other seven SAS men detailed to join the Det, were given training in a variety of new techniques that they might find necessary in their work. Andy particularly enjoyed the photographic sessions, learning how to use highly sensitive cameras, including infra-red equipment, and how to take pictures of photographs. On one occasion he returned home with a black and white aerial photograph of our new house which he had taken from a helicopter. The photograph was so sharp that I could see the house number on our wall and the detail of Jo's baby toys spread out in the back garden.

The soldiers detailed to serve with the Det were called 'Walts', short for the famous fictional character Walter Mitty.

Andy objected to the fact that he was ordered to go to Ireland and, for some unknown reason, fearful that he might be ribbed, called Walt by his SAS mates and treated as a Walter Mitty character rather than a macho SAS bloke.

'I'll deck the first man who calls me Walt,' he told me one day. And I'm sure he meant it. Yet to me it seemed odd that Andy should become so upset about a harmless nickname but, on the other hand, he always hated the thought that anyone could put him down, denting the image of himself.

For the six months leading up to their departure for Northern Ireland, the eight men were ordered to lead restricted lives. They were not permitted home during the week, and were even kept in camp over some weekends.

These restrictions, which the men considered unnecessary and petty, annoyed them intensely. Indeed, to segregate the Det men from the Hereford base they were stationed at Pontrilas, another SAS training camp ten miles from Hereford.

Their wives were also annoyed and upset that their

husbands were not allowed home during the week. One wife was expecting a baby and another, like me, had a young child, our husbands naturally wanted to see us and be with us. They knew they were facing the prospect of a two-year secondment to Northern Ireland and thought the SAS hierarchy most unfair and unsympathetic for not permitting them home at night, thus extending their forced separation from their families by a further six months.

So a plan was devised. Most nights the wives would take it in turns, on a strict rota basis, to drive to Pontrilas and pick up their husband for the night. The men would pretend they were going for a late-night run and the wife would wait in the car some distance from the main gate. When her husband drew level with the car, the wife would slow down to a walking pace, open the car door and he would leap in and lie on the back seat covered by a blanket for the drive home.

The next morning the husband, dressed in his running gear, would be dropped near the camp and he would run back in, pretending he was returning from an early morning jog.

That worked for several weeks until one husband was spotted. The eight men were called together and given the most almighty rollicking. They were also given strict orders that if anyone disobeyed and went home without permission they would face disciplinary action. The SAS didn't like to believe that any of their men would ever disobey an order.

One soldier, who hated the idea of spending two years in Northern Ireland working undercover, hatched a plot. Nearing the end of his stint at Pontrilas he deliberately broke the rules, ensuring that he would be discovered and was told he would be returned immediately to his Squadron. Overjoyed, he said farewell to his mates and returned home. The following day he was ordered to report to his superior officer at the main Hereford base. He was told he would be back on the next Det course, but would have to start again from the beginning. He had lost six months away from his family and friends.

The last few weekends Andy spent at home with Jo and me before setting off to Northern Ireland were emotional for both of us. He hated the thought that he would be leaving Jo for so long, that he would miss her first few steps, her first words and her first birthday.

Andy would say to me, 'You know that I don't want to go on this bloody job. I hate the thought of being away from you and Jo for so long, but we have no option. I'll ring you as often as possible but you must understand that it might not be every day. As soon as I know when I will get some leave, I want us all to have a wonderful holiday together, somewhere in the sun.'

There was nothing I could say to Andy to help him, but I could see that he would have difficulty in coping with the psychological stress of being away from us carrying out a dangerous and often boring job he didn't want to do.

I dreaded Andy's departure, not for his own safety, because I believed he was a first-rate SAS man capable of looking after himself, but for the psychological effect the job might have on him. I also worried about the repercussions of such a lengthy separation on our marriage.

I knew he would be on his own, carrying out surveillance work against the IRA, who would have no qualms about torturing and killing him if they ever discovered his real identity and that of his Regiment. And I also knew that he would hate being away from all his pals in the Squadron, the mates with whom he had enjoyed such fun and endured so many tough SAS training exercises.

Though I would speak to Andy by phone, usually once or twice a day, we would only see each other every three months, when he would be given either a five- or ten-day pass. Each time Andy flew back to Heathrow, I would drive down from Hereford with Jo to meet him and take him home. And the day before he was due to fly home, he would beseech me to make sure that I was dressed in an immaculate, brand-new outfit that he had not seen before. As ever, he would also ask me to wear my special kit — stockings and suspenders.

On one occasion, he was permitted to have 15 days' leave so we could all take a family holiday together. We flew to Tenerife with Jo in the spring of 1989, but instead of the holiday being a wonderful second honeymoon in the sun, enjoying time together with Jo, I sensed that our relationship was under some pressure.

Andy needed to spend time on his own, away from both Jo and me, as though the solitary surveillance work he was carrying out in Northern Ireland had made him used to his own company, his own thoughts. It seemed that he only wanted to be with Jo and me for short periods at a time, so very different from the man who had loved being together with us in our Hereford home before his enforced exile.

Before the Northern Ireland operation, Andy had been more talkative, more loving and more attentive, particularly towards Jo. Now, although on holiday, he wanted to spend time on long training runs, as though incapable of simply relaxing and winding down.

During that holiday, it seemed to me that Andy and I were simply going through the motions of being a happily married young couple in love with each other, our baby and the world. And yet I felt the strain beneath the surface and I began to feel a distance developing between us, even when we went to bed together after a lovely dinner and a few drinks.

We even argued about money during our holiday — Andy complained that I hadn't saved enough from the £240-a-month housekeeping allowance. Andy would tell me how he scrimped and saved in Ireland, surviving on little money, never going out on the town, hardly ever having a drink so that he never spent anything. And then he would point out that any money I had saved I would spend on myself and on Jo, rather than waiting to splash out on a great holiday.

'I do spend money on clothes,' I would argue, 'because you demand that every time you come home I'm wearing something new, something different.'

'That's peanuts,' he would say, 'what about all the rest of the money?'

I would tell him that I would have to pay the council tax, the gas and electricity bills, the insurance; that I had to eat and that Jo needed baby food and a constant supply of nappies. I would tell him that I never went out with the girls, except for the occasional coffee morning. I didn't drink in the pubs or go to discos. I would tell him that I was happy as a young mum staying at home and caring for Jo.

For 48 hours towards the end of our holiday, however, Andy and I once again became a couple of doting parents and happy lovers. Ironically, it was concern over Jo that brought us together. She fell ill and we had to call the doctor.

He diagnosed bronchitis and told us that we would have to monitor her temperature round the clock. Andy's mood and attitude changed within a split-second. He was brilliant, virtually never leaving Jo's bedside day or night. We would constantly cool her with cold towels; give her ice-cold baths; sit with her on the balcony so the night air would cool her. We both became very tired, but we knew we had to keep going for Jo's sake.

In the middle of the second night, Jo finally fell into a deep sleep and Andy and I fell fast asleep in each other's arms. When we awoke, still clothed and wrapped in each other's arms, we both realised that together we had helped Jo pull through.

From that moment, our holiday became more relaxed and I felt the happiness returning. We stopped bickering and started once again to enjoy each other's company. The passion returned to our relationship and we would fall asleep at night happy and relaxed. The days were spent caring and spoiling our beloved Jo.

But that brief interlude of exhilaration and inner

happiness would not survive Andy's two years in Northern Ireland, a period which seemed to drain the very spirit from our relationship.

He would continue to phone me each and every day, but the conversations would become shorter as we seemed to have so little to talk about. Understandably, he could tell me almost nothing of his surveillance work and I could hear in his voice the lack of interest in what he was being asked to carry out. Andy was usually enthusiastic about everything he touched or turned his hand to.

He could be the most wonderful company, always chatty and up-beat, often full of energy and ebullient, and to a woman he could be attentive, understanding, adoring and the most passionate of men. But two years in Northern Ireland took its toll on Andy and sapped his vigour and vitality.

I would try and interest him in what was going on at home. I would tell him about my new part-time career, making salt-dough decorations which I would sell to shops in Hereford. To me it seemed pathetic, talking of making and selling salt-dough figures when he was risking his very life keeping tabs on IRA gunmen and bombers. And, of course, I would tell him about Jo, of her progress and of the new little adventures in her life.

During the last nine months he was away, I buried myself in my small cottage industry, making perhaps twenty items a week. I felt proud that I was helping, in some small way, towards re-stocking the family vault, as well as continuing with my job at the Sun Valley factory.

But, in reality, I knew that I needed something to occupy my time and to take my mind off the empty days and nights without Andy.

Two years is a long time to wait and, although we would see each other every few months, we knew it would only be for a matter of days before he would be flying off again to a job he did not like in a country which was grinding him down. Whenever he flew out from Heathrow to Belfast, my heart would go out to him because I knew he needed all his inner-strength to keep going back. When he was back with me, I would deliberately never raise the subject of Northern Ireland because I knew how much he hated it. The last thing Andy wanted when back in England with his family was to talk about his work.

One weekend after I had picked him up from Heathrow, we arrived back home in Hereford and I wanted to take him to the shop which had a window display of all my work.

'For fuck's sake, Frances,' he exploded, 'I've just arrived home. I'm shagged out and I don't want to go fucking looking in shop windows in Hereford. Can't we go later?'

I was about to remonstrate with him, to tell him that I thought he might be interested in my hobby. But I bit my lip and waited for him to raise the matter. I castigated myself for bringing up my salt-dough creations when he had just returned home, because I should have waited until he had rested and recuperated, recharged his batteries, played and cuddled his beloved Joanna and enjoyed some relaxation at home.

So I never mentioned the damn things again, and neither did he. He would never see my display and that hurt me a little, but I blamed myself for having been so stupid and insensitive to the way he must have felt at that time, driving home from another few bloody awful months away.

That was a small, insignificant matter, but it seemed a turning point. I sensed that Andy was growing away from me, because he appeared to have little interest whatsoever in my life or what I was doing, only asking questions on the phone about Joanna and never about me, my work, my friends, my interests or our home. Always, when in such down-beat moods, I would mull over the situation, tell myself that I was worrying about our relationship because I had nothing better to do, and chastise myself for reading more into conversations and casual comments than was probably intended. But the nagging doubts continued.

In a bid to rekindle the love and the passion we had enjoyed at the beginning of our relationship, I persuaded my mother to take care of Jo for ten days while Andy and I 'got away from it all' and escaped to the sun for what I hoped would be another honeymoon. Andy and I spent ten days in Gran Canaria and had another ten-day holiday in the United States, spending three days in New York and a week in the warmth of Florida.

I looked forward to those holidays together. We both tried to enjoy our time together, but it seemed that we were both straining to enjoy ourselves, rather than actually doing so without forcing the pace. Andy would sometimes seem tired and listless and I understood that he needed to relax, sleep and revive his enthusiasm for the job he had to finish back in Northern Ireland.

Yet, in reality, it seemed we were only going through the motions mechanically, for there would be little buzz or sexual excitement between us, no passion or real love, and the tenderness that had always been there had somehow turned to boredom. That feeling imbued every activity we did together: having breakfast, going for a walk, enjoying a swim, wining and dining or even making love. As the days and nights passed, I hoped the love we had enjoyed in our early days together would return, but as the days ticked by I found little cause to rejoice. We had hardly spent time alone together since our wedding in October 1987, and now we found it difficult finding any loving enthusiasm for each other.

When we returned home, Andy told my mother about the holiday, saying, 'She dragged me around every bloody shop in New York. All she wanted to do was shop the whole bloody holiday.'

My mother looked at me and noted that I was not too happy with his reply. I was becoming more worried.

Our last holiday together was spent in Trevine, Cornwall, where Andy and I went to join my parents who had taken Jo with them. It would prove most embarrassing for poor Andy. My parents had given Andy a sail-board for a birthday present and he was keen to tackle the new challenge.

Andy didn't want to wear the traditional wet-suit and decided to ride the waves wearing just shorts and a T-shirt. He had never attempted wind-surfing before and my parents, grandfather and Jo were all on the beach watching him. It was a cold, windy day. At first, Andy practised near the shore line and it was obvious to us that he had no idea what he was doing. He had never taken lessons and seemed to be floundering. He would fall into the water every other minute and would scramble back on board with difficulty, requiring all his strength, energy and dexterity to get back up and set off once more.

Andy, however, seemed unaware that the tide had turned and he was being taken further out to sea. My father shouted to him, asking if he was OK, and each time Andy would yell back saying that he was in fine shape and needed no help. But my father became concerned when Andy appeared to be more than 400 yards from the shore in the middle of Padstow sound. Andy began to wave and we waved back thinking that he was just being friendly, enjoying himself. But he wasn't. Andy was in trouble.

My father went to seek help because he had become convinced that Andy was now in serious difficulties. A volunteer lifeguard, a man in his 60s, had also realised that Andy could be in trouble and asked a fisherman to go to the rescue. The fisherman chugged off in his fishing smack and 15 minutes later returned to the shore bringing Andy and his sail-board with him. Andy was freezing cold, exhausted and highly embarrassed.

The lifeguard said to my father, 'This is not a good spot for wind-surfing at the best of times. I had been watching him and knew he would be in real trouble if someone hadn't rescued him. In any case, he should never have gone out when the tide was approaching full ebb.'

Andy returned to Northern Ireland and the phonecalls back home became less frequent. I had high hopes that when his tour of duty ended in late 1989, and Andy returned home, we would be able to put our marriage back together again, start afresh and begin to enjoy a normal married life together.

Andy expected to be promoted to Sergeant in early 1990, which we both realised would mean a considerable pay-rise. I also looked forward to enjoying the camaraderie of the Sergeants' Mess as well as the more formal occasions and parties enjoyed by the SAS Sergeants and their families.

But Andy's return home from Northern Ireland would not turn out to be the second honeymoon I had planned. Andy appeared to be keener on keeping fit, going to camp and spending his off-duty time at a gym in Hereford run by a former Regiment man.

In the weeks and months before that fateful day in August 1990, when Andy told me our marriage was over, he would spend more time away from the house, not only during the day but also in the evenings, drinking with his former mates.

He returned after a long weekend away on a training exercise and, as usual, I went outside to greet him as he parked the car. I went to kiss him but instead of giving me the customary 'hello' kiss, he quickly bent down and picked up his bag, almost ignoring me. I followed him into the house. But he didn't want to know me, dropping his bags and walking into the kitchen to make himself a mug of tea.

I knew something dramatic had happened because Andy had never behaved in such an off-hand manner when he returned home, no matter how shattered he felt. I kept my distance and kept quiet, hoping that, in time, his mood would change and he would confide in me.

But the atmosphere remained strained and unnatural. Andy didn't say a word to me, neither did he make any move to kiss or hold or cuddle me. Throughout that evening, I wondered what on earth could have happened to cause Andy to cut me off in such a hurtful way and I sensed open hostility.

He told me he was tired and needed an early night, and I turned off the lights and went to join him. As I lay in the dark next to him, he made no attempt to touch or kiss me, or even to say 'goodnight'.

'What's going on, Andy?' I asked.

'Nothing,' he replied, 'I'm just tired.'

'No,' I answered, 'Something's up.'

There was a moment's silence. Then he said, 'Frances, I don't love you any more.'

I said nothing, struck dumb by this bald statement.

Receiving no response, he said a few moments later, 'But don't worry, it's probably only a phase.'

With that I got out of bed, went downstairs and made myself a cup of tea. I needed to think. I went into the living-room, sat on the sofa and pulled Jo's baby blanket over me to keep warm. Without realising what was happening, I felt the tears on my cheeks and I let them flow, feeling lonely and unwanted.

Minutes later, I could have laughed out loud in frustration and hopelessness because I suddenly heard

Andy snoring away upstairs in bed, totally and utterly oblivious to my thoughts of desperation and my feelings of abandonment.

The following morning, I bumped into Andy as I walked upstairs to see to Jo. We hardly said a word and he didn't look at me. He simply announced that he was off to work and was gone within minutes.

During the following week, I saw Andy each morning and he would return home late at night. We would sleep together in the same bed every night and I would prepare meals for him, but only when he asked me to. Many evenings he arrived home late and said that he already eaten.

He would tell me he was fond of me, and that he loved Jo, but that he wanted his freedom, that he *needed* his freedom. He demanded time and space on his own, living alone, to concentrate completely on his army career without any family responsibilities to hamper his determination.

When I asked him what had brought this to a head, he blamed the pressure of working undercover in Northern Ireland, having to take risks on a daily basis and yet constantly thinking of his responsibilities to his family back home in England.

A week or so later, Andy told me he had decided to move back into camp.

'Why?' I asked. 'You can stay here.'

'No,' he replied, 'that's being unfair to you. It's simply delaying the inevitable. I think it's better if I move back into camp.'

'Do you want some time on your own, to think this

through?' I asked, believing that he might come to his senses in a few days.

'No,' he said, without adding another word.

I knew immediately, instinctively, that that moment signalled the end of our marriage. I knew Andy well enough to understand that if he made a statement like that he would never change his mind, whatever happened — he was that sort of man.

Andy said that he would return later that day to pack and collect his gear. As soon as I walked back inside the house I went upstairs and packed all his clothes and personal effects, putting everything into black bin-liners.

When he returned and saw everything packed, he said, 'You didn't have to pack for me.'

'Yes, I did,' I told him, 'I couldn't have stood by and watch you move out all your clothes. That would have been too much to take.'

With that he loaded the car and drove away.

During the following week, Andy returned each afternoon at about 3.00pm. when I was due to return home from work having picked up Jo from play school. He told me that he came to play with Jo, and yet during most of those afternoons he hardly ever played with her but spent the time following me around the house, talking to me, asking me questions.

It seemed that he was trying to make up his mind what he should do — stay away or move back home? He would talk about our house, the love that had gone into it and the times we had spent together with Jo. But by 5.00pm each day he had gone. There was also a rumour going round that he was seeing a girl named Jilly.

I knew in my heart that Andy had found another woman and I feared that our marriage was finished.

Yet I knew I would be unable to leave the matter up in the air. Part of me had to know what was going on, though I feared I would discover what I didn't want to hear.

That night I determined to discover the truth. I wondered if I had made a great mistake, if I had doubted Andy unfairly or if I had misread the signs in his behaviour towards me. I thought of all those possibilities, but in the depths of my heart there was no doubt. I knew.

I would tackle the other woman in her own home, see it all for myself, because I had convinced myself that simply by looking around her house I would be able to tell — she might disclose those little tell-tale signs that can reveal the truth of a situation.

I drove to Jilly's house and knocked on the door and, to my surprise and embarrassment, Andy answered.

I took a deep breath, but I held my ground, determined to carry out my mission. He seemed hesitant and nervous. I told him that I didn't want to speak to him — I had come to see Jilly. After some hesitation, he agreed to let me into the house to speak to her.

As Jilly and I sat down to talk, Andy walked back into the room.

'Out, Andy, out,' I said, 'leave us alone.'

I don't know where I gained the strength to speak to Andy like that, for I had never addressed him in such a way before, but I had to show him that that day I meant business.

Jilly looked composed, sitting opposite me in a black and white blouse, flared matching skirt, smart high heels and what, I presumed, were stockings and suspenders. I looked round the room for evidence. Lying on the radiator I saw a cream set of stockings and the tell-tale suspenders, the type that Andy had always loved me to wear. My heart sank. Jilly saw me take note of the stockings and suspenders and when she looked back at me her eyes betrayed her thoughts. At that moment we both knew the truth.

The very fact of Jilly's youth, her smart appearance, her immaculate hair, and those suspenders indicating her sexuality, made me feel instantly frumpy. I wondered how I must have appeared to her, a woman four years her elder, dressed in an old pair of jeans and a blouse, my hair wind-blown, wearing no make-up and with a look of desperation and sadness in my eyes. I must have seemed so very vulnerable and, I thought, no real competition.

Somehow, I conjured up the strength to continue. I told her, 'I've come round here to tell you that I'm wife number three and you could possibly be wife number four. I only wish that Debbie, his second wife, had come to warn me as I have come round to see you.'

In a matter-of-fact tone, Jilly replied, 'I know he's a born liar, but we're going to take it slowly and see what happens.'

That opening remark made me feel a little better, although it made me realise that Jilly was an intelligent young woman who would probably take no nonsense from Andy.

And, surprisingly, she told me some facts which I knew Andy would not have wanted her to reveal. She told me that she and Andy had been for a long weekend together in August to Abergavenny in Wales, confirming that they were, indeed, lovers.

I asked her if she loved him.

'Yes, very much so,' she replied with candour, and I could see the love in her eyes. I knew exactly how she felt because I, too, had felt the same way about him.

As we chatted a little while longer, I decided to repay Jilly's openness with honesty, so I told her that if she believed Andy ever wanted to return to Jo and me, then I would happily take him back.

'I can see that,' she said.

At that point Andy walked back inside. 'That's enough,' he said, 'I'm not having any more of this,' and looked at me, his eyes burning with bitterness.

I drove back home with Jo feeling great that I had found the strength and confidence to meet his lover face to face. At least I now knew where I stood. The weeks of worrying were finally over.

Jo and I returned home to a house which suddenly seemed empty. I felt alone and vulnerable, the security blanket under which I had enjoyed peace of mind for four years had been ripped away. I was a single mum with a daughter to care for.

During those first few weeks as a wife who felt deserted, I would spend most hours of the day and many sleepless nights wondering where I had gone wrong, what I had done to foul up the marriage, blaming myself for the breakdown that had left Jo without a full-time father.

I remembered that we had had our first major argument when I returned home with some curtains for the living-room, as well as a pair of matching lampshades and five cushions for the sofa. I had bought them from Marks & Spencer. Jo was then three months old and I felt that I was building a home for our family. Andy believed I was wasting money and that we should wait until we had money to 'burn' on such unimportant items.

Throughout our four years together, however, we never usually raised our voices to each other, even during the worst arguments. Neither of us shouted or raved when we disagreed, but would discuss the problem rationally. On occasions, of course, fed up with the direction the argument was going, Andy would simply walk away, put on earphones and listen to his music. At that time, his favourites were Kate Bush, The Jam, Blondie and Frankie Goes to Hollywood.

The second major row was also over money. After we decided to go to Tenerife on our first holiday with Jo, we discovered that the holiday would be more expensive than we had thought and this caused me huge problems.

The third argument concerned the need to rebuild the rear wall of the last house we bought together. We planned to replace the single door leading from the dining room to the garden with sliding patio doors. We received an initial quote for about £300, but when the builder took out the old door and the necessary brickwork he thought that we needed a reinforced steel joist above the doors, costing an extra £600. At the time,

Andy was away and so I decided to fund the £600 with a bank loan, which I agreed to repay at the rate of £50 a month from my earnings. I knew Andy would go berserk if I told him the cost involved, so I kept the loan secret. I feared another row so I kept quiet.

I had only two payments left to make when Andy discovered my dealings by leafing through my files in our desk while he was looking for something else. Andy saw my secret loan as a betrayal!

We argued and debated and Andy lost his temper, but he refused to believe that I had taken out the loan to stop him from worrying about money. I told him that as he was away at the time, I sorted out the problem to the best of my ability by taking full responsibility for the repayment of the loan. He totally disagreed and believed that I was guilty of treachery. He vowed that he would never trust me again, ever!

I worried that it had been my ambition to create a home for us that had caused the major rows in the marriage. I became convinced that I was probably at fault, that I should have waited patiently for him to make every decision about the house, deferred buying furniture and curtains, delayed any redecorating or whatever was necessary until we had saved more money. And yet, at the time, I believed I was taking the right decisions for the three of us, because I knew that Andy wanted to be proud of his home.

Sometime in September 1990, a month after Andy went to live with Jilly, I looked at myself in the bathroom mirror and realised that I had developed a 'neglected' appearance since Andy's departure. I had, of course, gone through the motions — showering and washing my hair, washing and ironing our clothes — but I preferred to spend all my time spoiling Jo rather than taking care of myself. I was still working at the factory earning money, but did not want to spend anything on myself.

Though I would ensure that Jo ate as well as she ever had, I didn't bother about myself, surviving on snacks, ready-made meals and packs of crisps. I also began smoking again. I had given up smoking shortly after I met Andy, who hated the very idea of anyone smoking cigarettes, particularly his girlfriend.

I looked in the mirror that day and didn't like what I saw. I felt old and looked old and I believed that my days of enjoying life again as a young, energetic woman with vitality and a personality had gone for ever. I doubted that any man would ever be attracted to me again.

All I had going for me was Jo, and I decided to dedicate my life to her and her happiness and forget all about men. I would have to live alone, because I knew that Andy would not want me giving myself to another man and he would hate the fact that a man had taken over his rôle of father to his beloved Joanna.

I believe it was the girls at work who encouraged me and saved me from my drab and boring life. They built my spirit and little by little my confidence returned. They talked to me of all the other women they knew who had been ditched by their 'old man', only to bounce back and find a far better man the second time round.

Slowly, they encouraged me to venture out. I had done nothing except care for Jo, go to work, return home with Jo and after putting her to bed and reading her a story, eat something on my lap in front of the television. Most of the time, I would not even take in the programme, but would think of Andy and Jilly together, having fun, eating together and making love as we had done.

My Scottish friend Sheila, married to an SAS man in G Squadron, knew exactly how I felt, for her husband had left her two months before Andy had walked out on me. She told me to get a grip of myself, buck my ideas up, start wearing make-up and dressing smartly as I had done before.

At first I didn't want to listen to her — I was happy in my misery, boring all my friends with the stories of my marriage breakdown, forgetting that most of the women I was talking to had all been through the same experience. They had all been married and were all either separated or divorced. They were also all ex-wives of SAS soldiers.

After several weeks, the therapy finally worked. Sheila offered to babysit Jo and I was persuaded to join a group of ex-wives who were going to have a few drinks in Hereford and perhaps afterwards move on to a disco. I liked the idea of going for a drink, but I wasn't too keen on going to a disco; I felt too much of a frump. I was also extremely self-conscious, a woman who had been unable to keep her man or her marriage together. I believed everyone would be looking at me, pointing at me and gossiping about me.

The first tentative drink was a Bacardi and Coke; so were the second and the third. At first I simply buried my head, looking at the floor or at my glass, not wanting to look anyone in the eye. But by the fourth Bacardi I began to feel better. I started to lift my head, to look around the room.

Within an hour, I found myself chatting to an SAS guy I had never seen before. He was handsome but too short for me, although I enjoyed his patter and his sense of humour. Suddenly I found myself laughing and realised that this was the first time I had actually laughed in two months. In that instant, I realised how stupid I had been to bury myself away, believing that I could never enjoy life again. It also made me realise that I would no longer consider running away, leaving Hereford and taking Jo to a strange environment.

At home that night I slept more soundly than I had done for weeks, happy in the knowledge that I was again surrounded by friends, that I could enjoy myself on my own without Andy and that somewhere in the future there was another life beckoning. But I wasn't yet sure that I would ever find happiness.

The following Saturday, Sheila once more offered to take Jo for the night, and I went out on the town again with my friends. But despite my initial bravura, I found I needed three or four Bacardis before I found the confidence to relax and look around. That night I did go on to the disco, but I felt out of place, an older woman surrounded by sexy, good-looking young nymphettes. In fact I was being stupid — most of the women there were older than me — but I only seemed to see the young glamorous ones.

Within weeks, a group of eight ex-wives had formed a sort of unofficial lonely-hearts club and we would meet at someone's house for pre-drink drinks. We were all short of cash and most of the others felt the same as I did, lacking in confidence and in need of an injection of 'Dutch courage'. Most nights we would all have a few shorts before going into town.

At the disco I found my popularity returning and I would dance with a number of guys, nearly all from the Regiment. Slightly smashed and in a day-dream I preferred the slow, smoochy music and the feeling of a man with his arms around me, as though comforting me, making me feel more secure. Within a short time, however, I found myself drinking too much, waking on Sunday mornings with a hangover and not liking the sight that greeted me in the mirror.

One night in Garters I met a tall, well-built rugby player, a Welshman named Hywel who was also in the Regiment. We had never met before and yet from the moment our eyes met I felt an immediate sexual attraction. It was the first time since Andy that I had found any man even remotely attractive. We danced and smooched, drank too much and, after a couple of hours, I let him kiss me. It seemed odd, strange somehow, and I felt awkward. We arranged a date for a week later, and when I walked into the quiet country pub where we agreed to meet he stood up, kissed me on the cheek and gave me a warm hug. From that moment I knew we would be lovers.

I believe Hywel saved my sanity. He made me realise that a separated wife, whose husband had left her for another woman, can enjoy life and not feel guilty. He was kind and gentle and understood that I would need to take things slowly, rebuild my confidence and learn to trust someone else. Over the following weeks I managed to regain my poise and confidence. Finally, we became lovers and I realised that I could enjoy sex with another man, someone who wasn't my husband.

We met mainly at weekends and, after a while, I came to rely on Hywel to sustain my self-esteem. He encouraged me to cast aside my grief and misgivings, my doubts and mistrust and to face my future. Slowly I came to believe in myself, and through him I gained the confidence to enjoy myself and a new, different sex life. After a while we would spend our time together having wild sex, everywhere and anywhere, and he made me forget my pain and anguish over Andy. He restored my confidence and I found a new spring in my step. More importantly, I also seemed to have far more fun with Jo because I was enjoying life more, relaxing and better able to cope with the circumstances.

But the affair did not last. Hywel worried that our relationship was becoming too serious and he did not want to risk his career by becoming involved with an SAS Sergeant's ex-wife, nor did he want the commitment of taking on another man's child. I respected him for that and we agreed to go our separate ways. But Hywel had proved a good and honest confidant who had helped me over one of the worst periods of my life and we remained good friends.

But my involvement with Hywel had rekindled my interest in men. I began to search for other men who could provide me with the same excitement. But when I failed to find them I would resort to spending my nights out drinking too much. I would make sure I had three or four stiff drinks before leaving home and would never refuse a drink when offered. I found myself looking at men when not completely sober and finding them sexually attractive. I would dance with them and accept their invitations to go back to their homes and would crash out after having sex with them, usually waking in the morning regretting the activities of the night before.

After a number of drinks I found myself wanting to spend the night with an SAS man, any SAS man, never wishing to return home alone at night, and desperate to be wanted, screwed by a man from the Regiment, as though I had no defence against their all-powerful sexuality. I would think of spending Saturday night and Sunday morning in the arms of an SAS soldier, perhaps someone I had never met before. I would want to give myself to him completely, letting him do whatever he wanted, using me and, if he liked, abusing my body. The very act of giving myself to a Regiment man, of having sex with a strong, muscular, athletic SAS man who wanted me, would become a drug and my appetite knew no bounds. Though I did not always enjoy the sex, I revelled in my abandonment.

Each Monday morning I would take Jo to school before going on to work, sometimes feeling great. At other times, however, I would feel ashamed and even disgusted with myself and my sexual needs. But as the week passed, I would once again look forward to the weekend ahead, spending Friday and Saturday nights drinking, dancing, having fun and finding an SAS soldier to screw me and dominate me.

It was Nigel, a non-SAS man, who rescued me from this slippery slope. Tall, good-looking, quiet and well-spoken with a soft Irish brogue and receding blond hair, Nigel seemed the last person with whom I would have an affair.

He was, however, another military man, an officer in the Intelligence Corps whom I met at The Paludrine one night when he was on duty, dressed in his fatigues. At first I paid him no attention whatsoever, but he asked for my telephone number. I thought he would never phone, but a week later he invited me for a drink.

For some reason, I didn't want to get smashed whenever we were out together. I would deliberately not have my usual drink or two before going out. We would have drinks together in lovely country pubs, dine out once or twice a week or go for long drives into Wales. We got on really well, but it would be three weeks after we met that we first went to bed together.

At first, he seemed more shy than I was. It was strange after knowing a number of SAS men to find a man somewhat embarrassed. But he showed me kindness and gentleness and I appreciated the way he behaved towards me. I had always thought that I would only crave the tension and macho behaviour of a seasoned SAS man, but Nigel introduced me to a different, more gentle side of life that I came to enjoy. We would make love for three hours at a time, though he never tried to prove himself or his masculinity. And, perhaps more important than any physical attribute, Nigel made me feel loved and wanted once again.

I felt that the worst months of my life were finally behind me, that I had plumbed the depths of despair and loneliness, and had survived. But there would be worse to come.

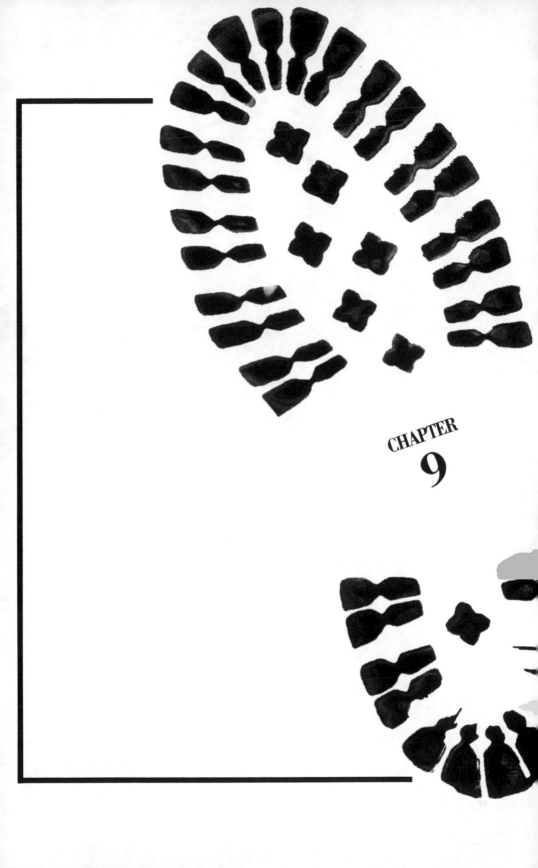

CHAPTER
9

'If I had married, I can t imagine
that it would have lasted, and I consider
the marriage vows to be very serious.'

COLONEL DAVID STIRLING

I AM NOT THE ONLY WOMAN to have won and lost a member of the SAS. I had never realised before Andy decided to leave me that there were so many ex-wives of SAS men. Many of them had left the Hereford area to start a new life away from the Regiment, in addition to the increasing numbers who could not wrench themselves away from the hot house of Hereford life.

Over the following two years I became good friends with a number of women, nearly all of them in their late 20s, who had married and had been dumped by their promiscuous young SAS husbands.

Without exception, all had tales to tell, mostly more horrendous than mine. We would talk about the way they had been treated and, more importantly, how they had managed to come to terms with the breakdown of their marriages.

Some wives would become so distraught that they would be admitted to the Jenny Lind Psychiatric Wing of Hereford County Hospital. Within hours, most wives on the Patch and those living around Hereford would have heard the news and the poor woman's marriage would be dissected down to the most intimate detail. And most wives would know in their hearts that the Regiment, the SAS lifestyle and the husband had all been responsible for the young woman's predicament.

Shortly after I moved to Hereford I met Barbara, a dark-haired, well-built young woman with a sweet smile and a sharp tongue, who had been married to an SAS man for four years. They had two children under three years of age and I would see the family most weekends going off together to the supermarket. Barbara and her husband John seemed ideally suited. But one night over a Christmas drink she disclosed the panic she was feeling.

Barbara told me that before they had married, John, whom she had met while he was in the Parachute Regiment, had twice left her for a former girlfriend after they had become engaged. They had married when she became pregnant, but she knew that John didn't really want to settle down. After the birth of their first child he had again left Barbara to return to his old flame, and she had managed for six months living alone in Hereford while he made up his mind about which woman he wanted to live with.

Eventually he had returned to her and, almost immediately, she became pregnant again. He walked out on her once more, but this time to live with a different woman, a nurse who lived nearby. Barbara told me how she had to walk past the house which John shared with the nurse most days, and how desperate and humiliated she would feel knowing they were there together, his car parked outside for the world to see.

Her mother came to stay for a week so that Barbara could have some time off, away from her two young boys. One evening she went out with some of her former girlfriends and had too much to drink. She hadn't had a drink for months and the alcohol went straight to her head.

She told me how she walked into the Queen's Head, a Regiment bar, and there she saw her husband passionately kissing his girlfriend. She lost control, ran over to him and hit him repeatedly on the back with her fists as she screamed obscenities at him. Then she fainted, an ambulance was called and after being admitted to the County Hospital she was transferred to the Psychiatric Wing.

'I don't remember anything of that night,' she told me, 'I don't remember what happened in the pub or why I collapsed. Some thought that John had hit me, but I'm sure he never did. I remember trying to behave correctly all the time, for I feared my boys would be taken from me and put into care.'

Barbara remained in the wing for two months before

finally being discharged. She told me how her husband pleaded to come back to her but she knew she could never trust him again and she refused all his requests. 'It was very, very hard,' she said, 'but the treatment at the hospital gave me the strength to live on my own without having to worry every night whether John would be coming home or not.'

Annie was a Regiment ex-wife whom I got to know particularly well because I would care for her on Saturdays when she was allowed out of the Jenny Lind Psychiatric Wing. I volunteered to help take her out shopping every Saturday in an effort to reintroduce her to society and restore her confidence which had been shattered by her husband's constant infidelity. I knew other ex-wives who had helped friends whose lives had been ruined by their relationships with men from the Regiment. Ex-wives who had survived marriage breakdowns would call the Psychiatric Wing offering help to those who had been devastated by their circumstances, so I decided to try and help someone.

Annie's husband, Mike, in his 30s, had been in the Regiment for eight years. He would return to Hereford from exercises and missions overseas but would stay at camp for two or three days, not wanting to return home immediately. Annie would sometimes hear from other wives that they had seen her husband around the town, and she would have to go to camp and ask why her husband had not returned with the other troops. Most of the time, she complained, the SAS would not want to become involved and she would be told that they had no idea where he was but that he was not in camp.

During that period, she knew that he was spending his time chasing and laying other women around Hereford, and she would hear from other wives that he had been seen drinking in pubs and dancing at discos.

On one occasion, when Annie believed her husband had returned from a trip, she waited outside the camp at dusk to watch him leave. She parked her car on the slip-road 150 yards from the main gate and waited. Within an hour she saw him drive out of the camp and she followed, keeping, what she hoped, was a discreet distance behind him.

She told me later, 'I followed him to a pub in the country feeling like some divorce detective. I waited outside and looked through the window. He was there with a young dark-haired woman who seemed to resemble me, only about seven years younger. I saw them kissing and touching each other. I followed them when they drove off in their respective cars. They parked in town and went to Garters. I saw them go in, their arms wrapped around each other.

'I debated whether I should confront him but I felt too embarrassed. I knew I would lose it and scream and cry and I didn't want people to see me like that. I went home to our empty house, because I had arranged for our seven-year-old to stay with friends. I saw no point in living and wanted to end it. I am sure that if I had owned an old-fashioned gas oven I would have killed myself, and I went to the bathroom and took out a bottle of aspirin. But I can hardly swallow pills at the best of times, and so that night I did nothing. When he breezed into the house two days later I was a terrible emotional state and he thought I had gone mad.'

Annie ended up in the clinic for a little over two months and her mother cared for her son. I looked forward to taking her out on Saturdays, buying her the odd new sweater and skirt to bolster her morale. We would talk about her problems over endless cups of tea and eventually Annie left Hereford with her son and went to live near her parents in Birmingham. She divorced her husband, but I believe they now have an amicable relationship and he does see his son.

I don't know if my small effort helped Annie, but I hope it did.

Valerie, a tall, slim woman nearing 40, the mother of three children, had been married for 15 unhappy years when she discovered her husband had been unfaithful to her. She believed that they had probably only spent four or five years together in total because he had spent so much time overseas and in Northern Ireland.

Valerie was not a strong woman and had spent many years of her marriage coping with her husband's drinking bouts. Whenever he came home on leave, he would spend most of the time in Hereford's bars and pubs drinking heavily, often being dropped off at home by a mate well after the pubs had closed. When he was at home during the day, still high on alcohol, he would take it out on Val and the kids, teasing, poking and gently punching them and demanding sex with Valerie in the middle of the afternoon when she was caring for the children.

One day she simply went to the medicine cupboard and swallowed all the pills in all the bottles, including her husband's drugs that he would take in the tropics. She was discovered by one of her children and taken to hospital, and her stomach was pumped. But the doctors believed that Valerie was in a critical condition and she was put on a heart monitor for 48 hours. After a few days, she was admitted to the Jenny Lind Wing and remained under close observation for several weeks.

Within a week, her husband, a Regiment Sergeant, had arranged for his children to be put into boarding school and then he went to see his wife. While she lay there under sedation he demanded an immediate divorce, announcing that he had taken custody of the children and that because of her stupidity in trying to commit suicide he would only permit her to see the children when it suited him.

It took Valerie three months to regain her strength and tackle the twin problems that lay ahead — putting her life back together and regaining custody of the three children she had devoted her life to bringing up. Eventually, her husband was persuaded to see sense and Valerie did win back her children. She would say later that she believed it took more than a few years for the children to come to terms with what had happened.

One source of information would be a nurse who worked in the Jenny Lind Wing who was also the wife of a Regiment soldier.

She told me, 'Understandably, I would learn the names of those Regiment wives admitted to the Wing very shortly after their arrival. Some would only stay for 48 hours, but many would need psychiatric treatment under sedation for some weeks. Others would be put under observation and lightly sedated and, hopefully, allowed to go home, though they would still need to take some drugs and return for regular psychiatric counselling.

'I cannot tell you how many SAS wives, and ex-wives, land up in the Psychiatric Wing, but there must be at least ten a year.'

Throughout all the horrendous stories of SAS marriages, however, perhaps the most heart-warming aspect was the remarkable relationship which developed between some of the SAS wives and, perhaps more importantly the ex-wives. Perhaps it was the natural tribal instinct the women felt, living similar lives with their husbands carrying out the same jobs in the same Regiment; perhaps it was the danger their husbands experienced which made them become a unified, understanding group of women, brought together by the common fear of their husbands being constantly liable to injury and possible death.

The wives, however, also fully realised that they shared an equally dangerous enemy — the shoals of young women who would frequent the bars and clubs of Hereford in search of a SAS man. We all knew why. The girls would be honest and open about the reasons: the SAS soldiers were on very good pay, led exciting, dangerous lives and had during the past few years, become publicly accepted as heroes. They were now the modern equivalent of knights in shining armour — strong, tough, daring, athletic, courageous and, *ipso facto*, highly sexy.

We, the women who were married to SAS men, knew that many teenage girls treated the SAS men as their local pop stars or soccer heroes, to be tracked down in their pubs and clubs and preyed upon. We would see the young girls out hunting their man every Friday and Saturday night, dressed in their sexiest outfits, trying to act older than their years, all drinking strong liquor, and discussing whether the objects of their attention were definitely SAS men. These girls were known to break off during a dance or a conversation if they discovered the young man they were chatting to was not a member of the SAS.

But the wives would stick together and the ex-wives would become even closer, supporting and helping each other in every way possible.

Hazel, a London girl in her 30s, had married Terry when he was in the Paras. I saw photographs of them together and Hazel had been a beautiful girl with a great figure and a pretty face. They seemed a wonderful couple who loved staying in every Saturday night in the winter to make love in front of the fire.

Young Hazel did everything. She not only decorated the house and made curtains, but also brought up the two children, as well as finding time to tend the garden and service their cars!

Some time after joining the Regiment, however, Terry began staying out late. And while Hazel stayed at home babysitting every night, Terry would be out, apparently with his mates in Hereford or in camp.

She discovered he was having affairs when she found love letters and Valentine cards at the bottom of a chest of drawers. So she decided to accompany him on nights out, sometimes taking the children with them.

She told me, 'Whenever we were out with the children, Terry and his mates would be drinking at the bar while I would spend the entire time looking after my kids. They rarely looked to their father for attention, presumably because they didn't see him often enough.'

Many wives would complain that their SAS husbands didn't see enough of their children. The wives understood when the men were away on exercises and missions, but most of the men seemed to prefer life at camp or in pubs when they returned home to Hereford, rather than staying at home with the wife and kids.

Terry began staying out late and drinking more, arriving home most nights abusive and barely able to walk straight. Though he was more than 6ft 2in tall and Hazel measured only 5ft 4in, she would occasionally physically throw him out of the house, locking all the doors until he returned sober.

Then he started to become mean with money. He would hand over only £40 a week to pay the bills and feed and clothe the children, saying he had no more money. Once, when her husband was away on exercise, she went to see the Families' Officer for advice.

When Terry returned and was called to see the officer he went berserk, terrifying Hazel and threatening to put her in hospital. She became so worried she could not sleep and her local GP prescribed tranquillisers. Angry and humiliated, Terry soon stopped paying the mortgage and Hazel discovered that her cheque book had been stolen, as well as all the money from the children's piggy banks.

Finally, Terry moved out altogether and the house

was repossessed. Hazel and the two children moved into council accommodation, but they had only the bare necessities. After ten years of marriage, Hazel and the kids had nothing. The ex-wives, however, heard of her plight and came to the rescue. They cleaned and scrubbed the entire house. They found carpets for the bare floors, picked up furniture and beds, provided sheets and old blankets, and found cutlery and china.

Three months after moving into her council house, Hazel had been persuaded by some ex-wives to join them on a girls' night out — a few drinks and a pizza. They clubbed together to pay her share. She had no clothes to wear, no make up, no stockings and no high-heeled shoes, so everyone chipped in. Someone provided a short skirt, someone else a top, others helped with make-up. Hazel looked great.

Unbelievably, her husband Terry walked into the pub where we were all drinking — she hadn't seen him for weeks. He had obviously had a few drinks. For some time he stared at her and she sought refuge amongst us, fearing he might become boisterous or, worse still, violent. Eventually, he came over and told her how sexy and wonderful she looked, and he invited her for a drink.

'Fuck off!' she said. 'Fuck off!'

It was the first time he had ever heard her swear.

She said later, 'Now I feel terrific. I've been wanting to say that to him for months, and now I've done it. And for the rest of the evening I'm going to make sure I have my back to him, 'cos I never want to see the bastard again.'

There were other occasions when the SAS ex-wives rallied round.

Tracy, a rather plump, pretty young SAS wife in her early 20s with long, straggly hair who never seemed to care a great deal about her appearance, lived for her baby and her husband, Darren. She adored him, a young, squat SAS soldier who sported a crew-cut hairstyle. She would do anything for him, buying him little presents every week, although she would buy very little for herself. After only two years of married life, she returned home one day to find a 'Dear John' letter on the kitchen table.

He wrote how sorry he was to leave her and their baby girl, but he had met someone else and had fallen in love. He would keep in touch.

Distraught and near-suicidal, Tracy talked for hours to the group of ex-wives who rallied round to help her. And then Darren began to visit her, to play with their daughter. And he began to stay for a meal, every so often.

The Ex-Wives Club decided that Darren could be persuaded to return home and three of them went to see Tracy.

'All we want to know, Tracy,' one asked her, 'is the answer to one question: do you want Darren back?'

'Yes, yes, yes,' she said between the tears.

'We think that he is showing signs that he may have made a mistake by walking out,' one explained. 'And we think we could help.'

'How?' she asked. 'How can you help? He doesn't want me any more.'

She agreed to take their advice. They took her to a hairdresser who changed her style, made her buy some new clothes and shoes, and showed her how to apply her make-up. On the night that Darren was due to see her, one took the baby girl for the evening and left behind a bottle of red wine. The metamorphosis worked better than they had planned. He took her out that night for a quiet drink in a pub and asked whether she would take him back. A little over nine months later, they had a little boy and he decided to leave the Regiment and move away from Hereford.

But for every success there were more than half-a-dozen failures. Some relationships would break up and the couple would get back together again, not once but sometimes three or four times.

One well-endowed SAS wife, an Irish girl with curly light-brown hair and a strong personality, called Sheena, agreed to her errant husband returning to the family home five times! She knew her husband Dick had been having an affair for several months, but he had always denied it. One day he phoned and said he had been detained and would return the next morning. Accidentally, though, he had not replaced the phone correctly and when Sheena went to use the phone seconds later she could hear voices. She could hear her husband's voice quite plainly and then a woman's voice demanding to know whether he had told his wife that he was going to leave her!

When he returned the next morning, Sheena was sweet and loving, making him breakfast and a pot of tea, fussing around him. The she asked him a question:

'Have you decided when you're going to tell your wife you're going to leave her?'

'What?' he said, his food exploding from his mouth. 'What did you say?'

'You heard me,' she said. 'Now tell me the answer.'

He left the table, came over to her, protested his innocence and tried everything to persuade her that he had not the slightest idea what she was talking about.

Then she told him of the conversation she had overheard.

'You would have thought I put a red hot poker up his backside,' she said. And before he could think of a reply, she said, 'Now stop your dirty lies and tell your wife the truth for once.'

He did, and he left within the hour, taking all his clothes. But he left behind all his SAS memorabilia, his SAS photographs, and the famous Regimental 'Stand By, Stand By' print.

But he would be back. Five times he returned and five times he left, sometimes staying a few days and sometimes a few months. However, within two weeks of his last departure, Sheena discovered that she was pregnant. She determined to keep the baby and Dick said that he would stand by her.

During her pregnancy Dick was due to leave the Army and was handed a handsome gratuity cheque for £30,000. He gave Sheena the lot. Together they bought a brand-new car for Sheena, and they went shopping together, buying furniture for the house and clothes for Sheena and the baby. Many ex-wives believed that Sheena and Dick had sorted out their problems and would stay together.

But before their daughter was born, Dick fled once

more and Sheena knew that he would never return.

What she had never considered was the phonecall she received from the girlfriend's mother, who told her how miserable and unhappy her daughter was because Sheena had been given all Dick's gratuity and had spent the lot! His girlfriend would become even more irate when she learned that her boyfriend Dick had even agreed to hand over the family home to Sheena and the children. And ever since Dick has tried to see as much as possible of his children, as well as maintaining regular, substantial maintenance payments.

Some ex-wives, however, would become so angry they would seek revenge!

I was sitting with five other ex-wives having coffee and listening to confessions when a quiet, shy woman in her late 20s, who had been married to an SAS man for six years, piped up unexpectedly. Karen hardly ever spoke during our coffee mornings but we would always invite her along because we felt rather sorry for her. She would dress in a rather plain, old-fashioned way, preferring skirts and dresses to jeans, and would wear hardly any make-up. Her hair was always swept back into a pony tail, tied with nothing more than an elastic band.

'I've been bad, too,' she said, and the group fell silent wondering what venal sin Karen could ever have committed.

One of the girls who often took the lead in our fireside chats encouraged Karen to speak out. I remember looking around the group as Karen told her tale. We were all riveted.

'You know that Bob left me,' she began, 'and that was

nearly a year ago. You know he told me that he was just going away for a weekend exercise and that he never came back. He even sneaked home and took all his clothes when I wasn't there. He only phoned me after being away a month but I told no one. Well, I waited for him to return, crying myself to sleep every night.

'Each day I seemed to hate him more for what he had done to me, walking out without saying a word, leaving me without a penny, clearing out our joint bank account. So I decided to get my own back. He had always complained that I hadn't been exciting enough for him, that I didn't do things other girls had done in the past.

'So I began phoning his fellow Sergeants, the old Regiment sweats who were older and more experienced than Bob. I would arrange to meet them, on their own, in out-of-the-way pubs, and over a few drinks I would leave little doubt in their minds that I fancied them, that I wanted to sleep with them.

'Only one out of seven refused to bonk me. One said he didn't want to know, so I spiked his lager with a whisky. That did the trick. But I only bonked each one once, and when we had finished I told them that I had only done it to spite Bob. I had been a virgin when Bob and I met, and he never thought in his wildest dreams that I would ever go with any other Regiment man.'

As she finished her story she looked at the floor, 'And now I walk around smiling because I know there are six other men, all Bob's friends, knowing that I have not remained faithful to him. One day I'll tell him, but not yet.'

A young wife in her late 20s called Sîan, a slim, short-haired blonde from the Home Counties, had been married for three years when her SAS man, a Sergeant named Keith, walked out after their marriage became a little dull. Sîan, who worked in a building society in Hereford, told me one night over a few drinks of her extraordinary sex life after her husband Barry had told her that their sex life was boring and pathetic.

'He never wanted to do anything out of the ordinary,' she told me. 'Our sex life had been good in the first few months but quickly became boring. He never wanted to experiment, he never even liked doing it downstairs or outside, in the car or standing in the kitchen.

'I had always wanted to experiment sexually, prepared to try anything and, one night in a pub in Worcester, I met an older man. He was in his early 40s, slim, quite tall, grey-haired and had dark, penetrating, very sexy eyes which made me go weak at the knees. He had been married and was now living with another woman, but he just seemed extraordinarily sexy. The moment we spoke, I knew I wanted him.

'Within a matter of days we were doing everything I had always dreamed of, but never dared mention to Keith. We made love in the car, over the bonnet of the car and on a rug in woods where we could see cars roaring past down country lanes.

'It was then that I found I enjoyed the darker side of sex which I had only read about. He wanted to tie me up in bed and screw me and I would let him. He would tie my hands to the headboard and spread my legs, tying my ankles to the bed-posts. Then he would take me, screwing me for a while and then leaving me, returning and screwing me again. It was fantastic.

'One night he asked if he could beat me with his belt and I agreed as long as he didn't hit me too hard. He began beating me and the harder he hit me the more randy I became until I was dying for him to stop beating me and start screwing me. After we screwed for a while he would stop, pick up his belt and start beating me again.'

Sîan told me how her lover bought a riding crop to make sure he marked her backside and that for the three months they remained lovers she always had the marks of the riding crop on her bottom. 'I would look at them in the mirror and feel instantly sexy. He would hit me a few times with the crop, sometimes really hard, and I would become so sexually excited I could hardly wait for him to start screwing me.

'The main reason I'm telling you this is not only because I want to share my secrets with someone, but also to say that, while all this was going on, I met Keith one night and we sat and had a drink. He told me how alive and sexy he found me, and asked what my secret was for looking so good.

'I was tempted to tell him that if he saw me naked then he would see my backside marked with 20 or more black, blue and yellow stripes, and that I was expecting more that night. But I didn't. I just told him I had found a new man who excited me. He looked totally disconsolate, for in those few words I had damaged his fragile ego. It made me realise how lucky I had been to escape from that marriage.'

There were also stories that depicted the hatred that

lay at the heart of so many broken relationships, but some had amusing outcomes as the violent husbands got their comeuppance.

Joan was in her late 20s. She was shy, quiet and well-built but she had shoulder-length fair hair that was always perfectly groomed and she dressed well, always looking attractive though never ostentatious. Joan's SAS husband, who had been in the Parachute Regiment, a six-footer with a strong, athletic body, believed he was one of the toughest men in the SAS. He would boast that he had never lost a fight in his life, whether among mates, in pub brawls or mixing it with people who wanted to have a go.

Joan told us, though, that he was also a bully, especially when he had had a few too many pints of lager. Then he would come home the worse for wear, if not actually drunk, and wake the kids and make them kiss him. If they didn't do as he said, he would slap them around a bit, making sure he hurt them and reduce them to tears.

'Then he would start on me,' Joan said. 'When he was in an aggressive, drunken mood he would demand that I did everything to him while he lay there on the bed, his arms behind his head, telling me I had to work on him for an hour or more if necessary until he became aroused. I used to hate that and he knew it.'

He finally left Joan and her two sons after one Christmas binge when he became so drunk he couldn't stand up. He arrived home on Christmas Eve, pulled the children out of bed, opened their presents and told them that there was no such person as Santa Claus. He told them that he bought their presents and because they had been badly behaved he was taking them back to the shop in the morning. He collapsed into bed, woke at midday and went drinking. He returned drunk, beat up the children and left Joan with two black eyes. Then he walked out swearing he would never return.

Joan began speaking quietly, making sure no one could overhear. 'But he only had a small willy and that embarrassed him. I think the size of his willy was one of the reasons he was so arrogant and domineering. So I decided to let his little secret out of the bag.

'I slept around a bit with a few of the lads who had always fancied me, and everyone I slept with I remarked on the size of their willy, telling them how small my former husband was in comparison. But I wasn't finished yet.

'After a few months, when I knew the word would have got round, I would sometimes see him chatting up some woman in a pub and I would wave to him with my little finger, making sure his lady friend could see what I meant. He would become furious and turn away, but he could do nothing about it. He never lived it down. In fact, a couple of years after constant teasing by his mates, he decided to quit the SAS and move away from Hereford. I never heard of him again, thank God. I never regretted what I did. He deserved it.'

There would be a number of other wives who determined to seek revenge on cheating husbands.

Ginny was a well-rounded, dark-haired Scottish woman, as well as being sharp-tongued and quick-witted. Her husband Alan had married her when she discovered she was three months pregnant. They stayed together for some time and they had another child.

But Ginny discovered later that even on their wedding day her husband found the time to bonk an old flame during the wedding reception.

'He would have sex with anyone who showed him the slightest interest,' Ginny said. 'I didn't realise at first that he wasn't at camp training or working. Most of the time he was with some floosie in some pub away from Hereford, chatting to her and then having sex somewhere or other.

'I challenged him about it one day and he told me, bold as brass, that all his mates had girlfriends on the side. He told me it was an open secret and none of the other wives minded. I told him that I minded, I minded very much, and he told me I had to take it or leave it. I thought about it for some time, but then I asked him to stop seeing the other women — he refused. So I told him to clear off out of my sight.

'He was gone the next morning, but he left behind his clothes and his belongings. I found out later that he had cleared out our joint bank account and he had even taken all the kids' savings.

'That made me see red,' she went on, 'so I ripped up all his army uniforms, his fatigues, everything and took them to camp. He had his name on all his gear so I just threw them on to the perimeter fence near the Sergeants' Mess so everyone could see them hanging on the barbed wire. I collected his books and wrote the names of every girl I thought he had ever known on the pages of the books. Then I gave them to the Families' Officer to give to him.'

Although Ginny had enjoyed her moment of revenge, she would lead a quiet, introspective life, working, looking after the kids and staying at home most evenings, never wanting to join our nights on the town.

She would say, 'I had my marriage. It lasted a few years and not as long as it should, but that was my luck. He's gone and good riddance to him. I wouldn't have him back if he begged on all fours.'

There were also some amusing episodes which we would laugh at in the telling.

Lovely Lee, 24, was short, petite, attractive and had short blond hair. Her husband Robbie, a former REME (Royal Electrical and Mechanical Engineers) man before being 'badged', was both a drinker and a gambler.

In her Cockney accent, she would recount how he would come home in the early hours, often drunk as a skunk and with no money left in his pockets. 'He would tell me how he fell into bad company, how his mates set out to get him drunk and then took him off to play cards. He would always have a bad luck story of how he was ripped off, cheated of winnings and had his drink spiked by other SAS mates who loved to see him falling around, drunk.

'But when he was at home and sober he was fine — kind and loving to me, but drunk more nights than he was sober. It became a difficult, almost impossible life.

'One night he came home and knocked at the door. I was asleep. It was 2.00am. I presumed he had lost his key so I went downstairs to see him standing there with a great big, live white swan tucked under his arm.

' "Ssshh," he said, looking around in case anyone should overhear. He could hardly speak but kept telling me that as he had lost all his money he had decided to bring home the Sunday dinner and he had caught the duck in the river.

' "That's no duck," ' I shouted at him, "that's a fucking swan you've caught, you great oaf. And if I'm not mistaken, the Queen could have your head chopped off for stealing one of Her Majesty's royal swans."

'He looked bemused, examining the swan closely as though trying to reach a conclusion. The swan and Robbie stared at each other as though both were deciding what to do.

' "Can you not cook it?" he kept asking.

' "No, I can't," I told him. "I'm not cooking some swan you've nicked from the river."

'So Robbie walked back 50 yards or so, put down the swan and staggered back inside. The last I saw was the swan ambling away down the centre of the road. I never knew what happened.'

Gordon and Marje were a Scottish couple who were well known in the Regiment for always bickering and arguing, even when they were out together having a drink and supposed to be enjoying themselves. Marje would tell the group about some of their arguments, always giving a wonderful twist to the tales, making them amusing and lively.

One of the best moments of her life was after a particular argument when she had criticised the Regiment and Gordon, a Glaswegian, had taken exception to her lambasting the SAS soldiers and their reputation for chasing women.

'Gordon would have none of it,' she explained, 'telling me they were the toughest fighting men in the world, the best trained and the most professional.

'The argument raged throughout lunch and I knew that a dozen SAS lads were coming over in Land Rovers to collect Gordon that afternoon. Deliberately, I tormented him until he became violent and he half-heartedly attempted to hit me. He had never done that before and I pretended to be awfully upset by his actions. As I heard the Land Rovers approaching I stormed outside, ripped off my wedding ring and threw it as far as I could into the neighbouring field.

'"What are you doing?" stormed Gordon. "That's the wedding ring I gave you — you can't throw it away."

'I walked to the car, got in, slammed the door and drove away. At the end of the road I stopped and turned round to see Gordon and his 12 men on hands and knees searching the field for my wedding ring. I roared with laughter and drove off. I returned some hours later and Gordon was there, triumphantly holding the wedding ring. We kissed and made up. It was not until two years later that I told him the whole episode had been a trick, for I wanted to see a dozen of the world's toughest men scrabbling around in the grass looking for my wedding ring. He roared with laughter. It was little episodes like that which kept our marriage together.

'I tell you young girls stories like that to show how artful you must be to keep these husbands guessing. Never let them get too big for their boots, and always keep one step ahead.'

And she would laugh at the memory.

But for increasing numbers of SAS wives, however, there would be no happy ending, no long marriages. Far too many would marry their SAS lovers on the spur of the moment or on the rebound, and for those who had married their men before they had joined the Regiment, they would find their husbands' personalities changing almost daily as they became subjected to the SAS way of life — the training, the exercises, the stress and the necessary commitment, as well as the attraction of readily available, younger girls who wanted to join the SAS mystique.

Audrey, a 23-year-old slip of a girl with long, dark hair, had only been married to her beloved Gary, himself only 25, for a few months when her sister Janice came to stay with them in their Hereford flat. They all got along famously and Janice returned for another visit that Christmas.

Audrey explained: 'A few weeks before Janice returned, I had found a pair of knickers under the mattress and I knew they weren't mine. I was out at work all day and decided to keep my eyes open but say nothing. I hoped Gary had simply enjoyed a brief fling, but I was angry that he had brought the tart back to our flat and they had obviously screwed in our bed. I watched and waited and saw no further evidence, and I would make sure that we made love nearly every night.

'The day my sister was due to arrive at Hereford, I decided to take the afternoon off and raced home to prepare a meal for the three of us that evening. I saw

Gary's car outside and when I went in I could hear the shower powering away upstairs. In the sitting-room I could see my sister's cases. I went upstairs and saw no one was around, so I opened the bathroom door. There, under the shower, were Gary and Janice bonking away. Janice was bending over the taps while Gary was behind, screwing her as the water cascaded over their bodies.'

'So what did you do?' I asked.

'I was in two minds,' she replied. 'Part of me wanted to shout out, but I felt empty inside. The fight seemed to have gone out of me, so I watched them for a while and then closed the door and waited in the bedroom for them to come out.

'They were laughing and giggling when they came out of the bathroom, but their mouths dropped open when they saw me sitting there. They were both stark naked. My sister ran back and grabbed a towel, and Gary tried to be all friendly and reassuring as though nothing had happened. He hadn't realised that I had seen everything.

'I told them that I had opened the door and I told them exactly what I had witnessed. My sister looked sheepish, apologising and saying they had just been carried away, that there was nothing in it, just a spot of fun.

'I didn't know what to do. Janice promised that nothing like that had happened before and would never happen again, and I convinced myself that Gary had probably instigated the whole affair. That Christmas was a very strained time for all of us, and it would be two years before Janice visited me again. In that time, however, Gary had become involved with various women around Hereford and I knew he was regularly being unfaithful. One day I suddenly decided I had had enough. I couldn't be bothered any more with his tarts and fancy ladies, so I told him to pack his bags and leave. He could see in my eyes and in my mood that there was no point in arguing, so he went upstairs, packed and was gone within the hour.'

But the strong-willed Audrey would be the exception. It seemed that most ex-wives would nearly always want their husbands back again no matter how badly they had been treated.

We would discuss such matters endlessly, wondering why we would take back our errant husbands. Many ex-wives believed the main reasons to be loneliness and unhappiness, having to survive on the little money dished out by the DSS, having to take all the responsibility for bringing up the family, running the house and eking out their meagre finances while trying to lead lives of their own.

All agreed that the support from other ex-wives helped tremendously. They would also become closely acquainted with the song that seemed to be on everyone's lips, Gloria Gaynor's 'I Will Survive'. Many wives would tell how they would put on that track and turn it up loud as they did their housework, hoping to boost their self-confidence. At discos, ex-wives would look knowingly at each other whenever that song was played and we would all, momentarily, be back in our homes, thinking of the bad times that had made that song so important to us.

*   *   *

The discussions among two or more ex-wives over a tea or coffee would invariably lead to an analysis of the men — the SAS soldiers with whom we had fallen in love and who seemed somehow incapable of leading normal family lives.

It seemed that the lifestyles of SAS soldiers were incompatible with settling into the routine of happily married men, able to sustain a loving relationship with a wife or partner.

It seemed that many of these men could not enjoy, or really understand, mature relationships with women, and they were unable to sustain their interest in one woman for very long. Many of us would feel that the men needed their women for sexual gratification and, more often than not, to boost their fragile egos. But for long-standing relationships they seemed to prefer each other's company. Many of us believed that our husbands needed to talk 'at' us, but wanted to talk 'with' each other, as though we were not capable of understanding their feelings and attitudes.

We recognised that our husbands had a need for the tribal security of a small, intimate group with total loyalty to each other. Like all soldiers, we understood that they were essentially gregarious men but function best in small, family-sized groups that do not swamp individuality.

We wondered whether the camaraderie encouraged so steadfastly throughout SAS training had such an effect on the men and their psychology that women, even their beloved wives and girlfriends, became almost superfluous. We knew Regiment wives were treated as second-class citizens, and were made to understand that their partners' devotion to duty and the Regiment was of paramount importance. We knew that their training drills, pushing a man to the very limit of his endurance, were designed to focus a man's mind to the task in hand, consigning everything else, including his family and his home, to the background.

We understood the Regiment's philosophy of punishing training, infusing every man privileged enough to be badged with a sense of being part of an élite military group willing to take the greatest risks.

I had read of the paper produced by Major Dare Newell in 1955, embodying the Regiment's basic philosophy: 'Selection is designed rather to find the individualist with a sense of self-discipline than the man who is primarily a good member of a team. For the self-disciplined individualist will always fit well into a team when team-work is required, but a man selected for team-work is by no means always suitable for work outside the team.'

We understood that the SAS looked for mature soldiers, usually over 25, with the relevant qualities to allow them to work for weeks and perhaps months in isolation. These qualities included initiative, self-discipline, independence, an ability to work unsupervised, stamina, patience and a sense of humour.

And yet it seemed to many of the SAS wives that these qualities were precisely the same as those needed for a happy, successful marriage. It seemed that the men, our husbands, were not capable of achieving and maintaining the same exacting standards at work and in the home.

Many wives would suggest that their SAS husbands were 'incorrigibly immature personalities', seeking to prove themselves against each other, as well as against the toughest training regime in the British Army. The wives would see that in the way the SAS troopers would want to prove themselves to other, younger, more attractive women, not simply to show off in front of their mates, but to prove to themselves they were the élite in all aspects of their lives. This included the ability to attract members of the opposite sex with a swagger in their walk, a come-hither look in their eye and a career which embodies that elusive element of sexual attraction — danger.

And yet we would all agree — girlfriends, wives and ex-wives alike — that there was something different, exciting, irresistible and challenging about being involved with an SAS soldier. We also all agreed that most were 'right bastards'.

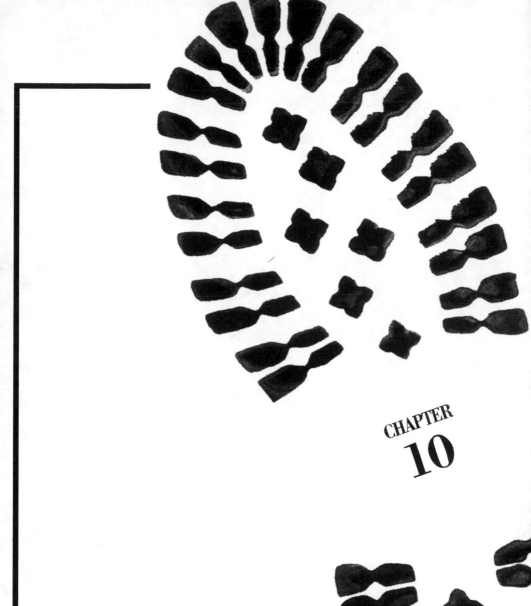

CHAPTER 10

**'All ranks in the SAS are of
'one company', in which a sense
of class is both alien and ludicrous.'**

COLONEL DAVID STIRLING

EVERY FEW MONTHS, all members of the Special Air Service
are routinely subjected to psychological tests conducted
in the camp by highly skilled medical personnel who
have no connection with the Regiment.

Some are asked to undergo these tests when they
return from long tours of duty, as Andy was when he
returned from his two-year stint in Northern Ireland.
These were also undertaken, of course, when the
Regiment returned from such missions as the Falklands
and the Gulf War.

I and many other wives believe the men need far

more help than they are given. They are apparently rigorously tested, but it seems that only if a man has serious psychological problems, or worse, possible disorders, will he be taken off duty and given the necessary treatment and counselling.

All SAS men are deeply troubled by the death in action of a close comrade. I saw a number of Regiment soldiers deeply hurt by the death of a mate. I have seen soldiers crying openly when talking over drinks at the death of another soldier from the same Squadron, and even more so of someone in the same Troop. And yet those who survived and made it back to Hereford are seemingly over their grief and their psychological trauma within a matter of days and no one mentions the subject again.

I do not know what happens during their chats with doctors after such grief-stricken events, but I do know that the SAS guys are encouraged to put their grief immediately behind them, to look forward to the future. It seems extraordinary that the SAS soldier seems, within days if not hours, to have overcome the grief for a comrade when only hours before they had been nearly sick with despair and grief over his death.

Drink, and to a lesser degree sex, is the way many SAS blokes seem to cope with the sadness and the loss. After the death of a colleague, the men will go out on the town in a group, drinking vast amounts of beer and lager, sometimes having whisky chasers, ensuring that they will be completely drunk for the rest of that night.

And there is little a wife or a girl friend can do to help them with their sorrow.

Only very few SAS men want to share their grief with their womenfolk. The vast majority want to get over the hurdle of despair with their mates, or keep their feelings to themselves.

It is at such times that all SAS wives feel superfluous, realising that the comfort they can provide and desperately want to give is not appreciated or requested. Those are hard times for the womenfolk because they feel they should be there for their grieving, sad, unhappy soul mates. But there presence is not wanted on such occasions, for it seems to be a time for men to mourn together. It is a lesson every young SAS wife must learn and learn quickly, as it is a hard, unnerving SAS tradition that has always been followed.

Time and again, every SAS wife has heard the same cry from their husbands: 'You have no idea what I'm going through. He was *my* mate, not yours. You can't understand. We were there together and he bought it and I didn't.'

There would be other SAS men who would never show the slightest mood change, entirely blocking out the emotions that everyone else suffers at that moment of deep personal crisis.

To show their companionship and their feelings of remorse, all mates and comrades will attend the famous auctions that take place after the death of an SAS man, selling off the dead man's clothes and personal belongings with all the money being handed over to the widow and children.

I have been told of men paying £100 for a pair of filthy, old trainers, £50 for an army handkerchief or scarf, all digging deep into their pockets to ensure that the widow has a pot of money to help her through the first few months of life alone.

The wives and ex-wives, though, will provide the widow with the emotional support she needs. They will gather round her, help her out in whatever way they can, ensure that she is never left to grieve alone and encourage her to attend all the social activities. Hopefully, she will be made to feel that despite the loss of her soldier husband, she is still very much a part of the Regiment. The everyday needs will be taken care of: shopping will be done, clothes will be picked up from the cleaners, errands will be run, and children will be looked after.

And the SAS men will leave the womenfolk to care for each other. Usually the men will not go round to see the widow, sit with her and answer whatever questions she may have, but instead they will prefer to keep their distance, not wanting to be too near someone grieving about a dead man just in case the feeling of sorrow and remorse is passed on. Death is a fact of life that an SAS man wants to run from, ignore and forget. And he does.

Those men who run the Regiment, who send the young, tough professionals on their daring and, sometimes dastardly, missions will send a representative to the home of the widow to talk things through, offer advice and sort out the financial affairs. But they seem to prefer the wives to care for the widows and each other. After an initial visit from the Families' Officer, there may be a follow up visit or two but the Regiment also wants to forget about failures or mistakes, like the accidents, injuries and fatalities that occasionally occur.

During the Falklands campaign and the Gulf War, a number of SAS men taking the greatest risks and operating with extreme courage were killed in action. Services of remembrance were held, the dead were buried and the churchmen offered prayers for their departed souls, but before their names had been inscribed on the Clock Tower at Stirling Lines, the soldiers who had fought by their side had pushed aside the memory of their dead comrades. For that is the tradition of the SAS, encouraged by their famous motto 'Who Dares Wins', a sentiment which never dwells on the faintest possibility that an SAS man could ever be killed in action.

Senior officers do not want their troops to fear that they, too, might be killed during the next tour of duty in Northern Ireland, the next real-life exercise in the jungles of Brunei or Indonesia, or, more likely, during the next skirmish in some God-forsaken area of the world which is never brought to public attention.

Young potential recruits train for months getting fit enough to take the SAS selection examination, running for tens of miles with Bergens filled with bricks. More than 90 per cent never finish the examination. If they pass, they are then subjected to six months of the toughest of training regimes. Many fall by the wayside and are instantly RTU'd. But if they pass they are finally badged, often thrown the sand-coloured beret by the Colonel and told, 'Remember, young man, this is easier to get than to keep.'

And yet such is the pride of wearing that sand-coloured beret with the SAS winged dagger, such is the psychological grip engendered by the training which never ceases throughout their time with the Regiment, that many SAS men do become impervious to the thought that any enemy will stop them, or kill them.

The SAS soldier does not think he is the best fighting machine in the world — he knows it.

This arrogance is also, unfortunately for their families, their attitude to life. They carry their training and their sky-high self-confidence into their private lives, and that has a disastrous effect on their attempts at married life, with more than 50 per cent of all SAS marriages ending in separation or divorce.

The girlfriends and wives, however, receive no training whatsoever in how to deal with these men and their inflated egos. Most SAS men do believe that they are superior to any other member of the forces and they tend to treat civilians as a lesser breed.

All SAS wives realise very shortly after their men have been badged that, in reality, they are dealing with the fragile ego of a child. They need absolute support and encouragement, their confidence needs to be boosted in every possible way, particularly between the sheets. Most wives know that their husbands are insecure and one of the reasons they have subjected themselves to the rigours of the SAS training course is to try and prove themselves, both physically and mentally.

And that state of mind continues, even appears to be encouraged, throughout their months and years with the Regiment. They never lose their super-egos, they know they have to be super-cool and totally collected at all times, and they practice that in every facet of their lives both on- and, more importantly, off-duty.

The wives are meant to understand all this. It is lucky for the Regiment that SAS wives take it upon themselves to talk to each other, visit each other's homes, and deliberately go out of their way to support each other, because the wives realise that their husbands generally behave in the same way. The husbands believe they are super-special, but they never seem to consider that their wives, who have to live with their egos and their self-delusion, are also special.

Of course, the wives do understand that their husbands face danger and must learn to cope with it as best they can. That is why wives try to keep everything calm at home before a Troop or Squadron are about to leave on active service. They know their men are hyped up, tense and thinking of the immediate future, no matter how many jokes are cracked and how matter-of-fact they appear to be as they kiss their wives 'goodbye' and walk through the door.

But every time Andy walked through that door, to go to Northern Ireland, or when he went to the Gulf War, I would always think that farewell might be the last time I would ever see him. It was not as though he was going to catch the 7.45 train to work every morning, no matter how positive a wife tries to be. He is going to face danger and possible death. All SAS wives think that, though they try to put a brave face on it and some pretend that they never suffer any anxiety on those occasions. But I doubt it.

I coped with my feelings by walking back into the house, going immediately to the dining-room table and starting to write my first letter to him, telling him how much Joanna and I missed him, hoping he was well and taking care of himself. And I made sure the letter was light and up-beat with no hint of the real reason I was writing, trying to calm myself and make myself believe that he would be back in just a couple of weeks.

I would spend the days worrying about him, where he was, what he was doing, and would look at Joanna and wonder if she would ever know her father or whether he would ever return to us. I would fuss around the house, rushing around keeping myself busy, trying to remember all the tiny items that needed attention, but only really to pass the time until he returned.

I would talk to Jo about Andy, even though she was only a baby, telling her all about him and that he would soon be home to play with her, bath her, wash her hair and take her for walks in the pram. She couldn't understand a word but it made me feel better. I would look into her big, pale-blue eyes, replicas of her father's, and think of Andy.

Whenever Andy returned home he would be wonderful with Joanna. But many wives would complain of major problems when their husbands came back after several months away. Sometimes, the younger children would not even recognise their fathers, especially if they walked into the house sporting a new beard.

Older wives would advise the younger ones with

children to try and prepare their offspring for their father's homecoming. One wife told us, when her husband walked into the house, his daughter, nearly a year old, took fright and hid behind the sofa, afraid to come out until he had been upstairs and shaved!

And all wives would talk bitterly of the problems caused when their husbands returned home and once again assumed command of the household. Because they had been used to military discipline and the most incredible self-discipline, they would expect their children to behave as they wished and demanded. The SAS men would expect their every word to be taken as an order and could not understand the more gentle discipline that had been going on in their absence between the mother and child.

As a result, many homecomings were ruined by the tense atmosphere in the house, when the soldier would discover that the children had minds and personalities of their own, which they had developed without their father's influence. They were now capable of showing off their new-found confidence to the father they hadn't seen for weeks or months.

The more mature fathers would understand such problems, but the younger men in their 20s, whose children were only toddlers or very young, found their childrens' independence difficult to fathom. More often than not the wife would get the blame and the homecoming which she tried to plan to perfection would dissolve into arguments, recriminations, disappointment and tears.

Many of the Hereford wives would complain that

within hours of walking through the front door their husbands would decide to go out again for a few beers with their mates.

The process of rehabilitating the relationship would sometimes only take a matter of hours, but for some couples days would go by before they had re-established a good relationship. Whenever children were involved, of course, the process would usually take longer and the problems would sometimes become more acute.

The older children would sometimes suffer deeper psychological problems, feeling happier in the freer, more open life at home when their fathers were away. They would become used to life with only their mother to discipline them. Home life was less formal without their father's presence and they were generally allowed the run of the house, often getting their own way.

Some children of SAS men, both boys and girls, would become awkward and troublesome at school, reacting poorly to school discipline and arguing with teachers. Such indiscipline would nearly always occur shortly after their fathers left on a trip. Having acquiesced to their father's wishes, they missed his company. Many SAS men spend between four and six months of every year away from home and this causes immense disruption in a child's psyche.

The one positive aspect for both wives and children, however, is that unlike other service men and women the SAS is always based at Hereford, so that children do have the emotional security of keeping their friends, attending the same school and having a permanent place they can call 'home'. Wives, too, can put down roots, make enduring friendships, join clubs and become known in the local community, as well as maintain a home where they know they will stay for several years. Many other service wives have to move house frequently uprooting their lives every two or three years.

That sense of belonging is one of the main reasons why ex-wives of SAS men don't move away from Hereford when their marriages break up. The ex-wives need their friends around them for support, as opposed to being cast out to start a new life in a strange town, without friends or family. There are frequent instances, though, of SAS men actively encouraging, and sometimes pressurising, their former wives to leave Hereford, to leave 'their town', so that they can get on with their lives without the constant presence of an ex-wife.

*   *   *

There had been some unfortunate incidents involving ex-wives who would deliberately visit The Paludrine to antagonise their former husbands and their new girlfriends.

One wonderful, unforgettable incident was always mentioned because, on this occasion, the ex-wife claimed victory. She had been drinking with friends in the club for sometime when her husband arrived with his girlfriend. He had already been warned by a mate on the gate that his wife was inside.

'No trouble, mate, OK?' he said.

'There'll be no bother,' the husband replied in his

broad Scottish accent.

Later that evening, the wife was sitting having a drink when she was unexpectedly joined by her former husband and his girlfriend. They chatted amicably for a little while and then the wife began telling the girlfriend some 'home truths' about her husband: the type of man he was; his demands and shortcomings; his short temper and big drinking. He objected and the wife saw red. She picked up his pint of lager and her drink and poured them over their heads. And then, before he could react, she punched him in the mouth.

The two soldiers on duty that night, whose job it was to ensure members behaved, grabbed the husband and his girlfriend and escorted them out of the club. There were cheers from those who witnessed the altercation and, overnight, the ex-wife became a heroine.

She would say later, 'It must have been the drink. I don't know how I had the courage to do it. I was shaking all over but something inside gave me the courage.'

Later, I heard that the SAS were seriously thinking of banning all ex-wives from The Paludrine because they caused embarrassment and unease for their former husbands. In fact, some years later the SAS decided to close the club altogether and, as a result, no girlfriends, wives or ex-wives attend weekly social gatherings in Stirling Lines.

And relationship problems did not stop with the vengeance of ex-wives. The authorities had discovered, much to their chagrin that, since the Falklands War, members of the SAS had become targets for young women who wanted to share their dangerous lives and

Top: Aerial operations in the Gulf War.

Below: Hundreds of Iraqis were killed on the Basra Road as they fled home at the end of the Gulf War.

Top: Me (back row, far right) aged 6 ½ at Alverstoke Infant School.

Below left: Young and single with friend Julie – I am on the right.

Below right: Seventies fashions…

At work with Giovanni, October 1978.

In Corfu, taking it easy with friend Denise, June 1978.

Top: Tanning on the rocks in Corfu, 1978.
Below: Sunnier days in London, 1996.

Jo with Andy's parents, Herefordshire, Summer 1989.

Jo with my parents Peter and Del, and Katie the dog, Hampshire, Autumn 1992.

Jo and Andy in happier times, Summer 1989.

hoped that the glamour would rub off on them, too, giving them an instant cache, a social standing above any of their mates.

What worried the authorities was the reaction of the young recruits once they had been badged. Many, whether married or not, found it difficult to turn their backs on the groups of young women who wanted to share in the 'glamour'. Most of the girls didn't seem to care a damn whether the objects of their attentions were married, engaged or single. The girls believed the SAS men to be fair game and would try everything in their power to capture an SAS scalp.

Many younger SAS blokes, unused to such adoration, loved the attention and the hero-worshipping girls, and were only too happy to drink and dance with them. They were also only too happy to enjoy the sex that always seemed on offer, with no questions asked.

But the number of separations and divorces escalated alarmingly and the SAS Families' Officers found increasing numbers of young ex-wives with babies and young children knocking at their door, asking the SAS to make sure their husbands cared for them and their children, paid regular maintenance and didn't simply dump them, move on to the next relationship and forget their family responsibilities.

It was one of the reasons why so many SAS men never wanted their former families to live in or around Hereford, but preferred them to go back to their parents, taking their children with them.

'Out of sight, out of mind' was the phrase I would hear so often from several ex-wives. It was also the reason that many refused to leave Hereford, so they could keep an eye on their ex-husbands, ensuring that he faced up to his responsibilities.

*   *   *

The unofficial 'Ex-Wives Club' was one group which actively tried to offer support in times of crisis. The help, advice and camaraderie the ex-wives received from each other seemed better than any official counselling. Everyone helped each other, the older women advising the younger ones how to play their errant husbands.

But there were many hardships, too.

To many ex-wives it seemed that the SAS authorities didn't want the embarrassment of ex-wives, and would go out of their way to comply with the wishes of the SAS soldiers, seemingly not caring a damn for the responsibilities they were shunning with such impunity.

Many ex-wives would find themselves in severe financial straits, but appeals to the SAS authorities would produce very little financial advice or assistance. It seemed to most ex-wives that the SAS officials had no wish to make their men face up to their family responsibilities. Most ex-wives would simply be advised to seek help from the Social Services, even though their husbands were earning good pay and allowances.

As a result, there were many impoverished and angry young mothers around Hereford who were expected to cope with their children, run a home and make ends meet with little or no help from their husbands.

Betty, the ex-wife of an SAS Sergeant, a large, well-built woman from the north of England, bore her husband three children. But a few months after the last baby was born, he moved out of the family home and went to live with a younger woman in a flat on the outskirts of Hereford. Betty had no job and no visible sign of support.

'I went to the Families' Officer and told him what had happened,' she explained. 'I told him that our marriage had been good but suddenly, when he was in his 30s, he had felt his life was flying past and he wanted to enjoy himself. I told the officer that my husband, Dave, had given me nothing since leaving the family home, and he refused to see me or discuss the matter. I asked whether part of his pay could be stopped and put into an account for me. They told me that that was impossible and that I should go to the DSS and apply for aid.'

Eventually, Betty managed to get a court order against her husband for the princely sum of £75 a week, to pay the rent, clothe and feed the three children and herself, and to pay all the bills.

Betty told me later, 'Of course, things steadily went down hill. I had terrible problems making ends meet. In fact, I couldn't, though God knows how I tried. And I would see Dave driving around Hereford in a nearly new car with his girlfriend dressed in new clothes, while I was struggling home with a pram, three kids and the shopping.

'It seemed despicable that the SAS would permit their men, who are very well paid, to turn their backs on their families and their responsibilities, and do not attempt to try and persuade them they should not behave in that way.'

Betty told me that on one occasion she had cornered an SAS officer and talked to him of her plight. He had said that, because of the dangerous nature of their missions, it was vital that the soldiers should be happy and settled, their minds focused on the job in hand not having to worry about family problems or relationships.

Many ex-wives had similar stories to tell. Nearly all their husbands had left behind one or two children and all had gone off with younger women, some much younger.

Janet, a girl from New Zealand who had married a soldier before he had been badged, told me of her plight. 'We had two wonderful sons in the space of three years and we married and settled down. Everything seemed great and Mick loved to spend all his time off and his leave with us. We had a lovely home, a mortgage, cosy dinners at night and I felt I was very fortunate, happy in a loving marriage. Then he began staying out late and I feared he had met someone else.

'I began to ask questions and he would become violent, telling me to shut up. If I persisted he would walk out of the house, slamming the door and not returning 'til the next morning. When I asked where he had spent the night he refused to tell me.'

A couple of weeks later, he informed Janet that he was leaving her. He took everything he owned, threw the lot into the car and drove off.

She went on: 'Distraught, I turned to friends and

some days later learned that he had moved into a flat with a teenage girl. He had said that he hadn't been happy at home for months and had found someone to love him.

'I checked our joint bank account and found he had removed the lot. There wasn't a penny left. I went to see the Families' Officer and, after listening to my story, he told me there was nothing he could do. I would have to sort out the problem with my husband. If I needed money, I would have to go to the DSS.

'I felt so bitter that the SAS hierarchy, who are meant to look after their soldiers, train them to peak fitness and send them out on the deadliest of missions, don't seem to care a damn about the soldiers' families, their children or their responsibilities. The only responsibility an SAS soldier has, according to his senior officers, is to his mates and his comrades, but not to his wife or family. That sort of attitude is despicable. One would think the SAS would instil in their men some responsibility towards their wives and children.'

Natalie, another SAS wife with two children, a boy and a girl, had only been married for two years when her husband walked out. They had married when she was pregnant with their first child and lived in a rented house near Stirling Lines.

A striking young woman of 25, most wives felt Natalie was a beautiful-looking woman though not tall. She also possessed a strong character and a sharp tongue, and would often stand in Hereford bars denouncing the SAS men around her.

She would find out as much dirt as possible about

various soldiers in her husband's Squadron and talk in a loud voice, making the men squirm with embarrassment. Many would ask her former husband to stop her, control her or shut her up. But she had no intention of being silenced. Her husband Bill had walked out on her for a younger woman, though someone nowhere near as glamorous as Natalie, and had refused to pay her any maintenance.

As a result, she would deliberately visit the pubs he frequented with his new 'floosie', as she called her to her face, and order drinks which she would refuse to pay for. Embarrassed, angry and feeling compromised, Bill would reluctantly pick up the tab.

'His pride and joy,' Natalie said, 'was his bloody car, a two-year-old Volkswagen Golf that he would clean and polish every week. When he returned from exercises having been away two or three weeks, he would spend two minutes in bed with me, giving me a quick one, before getting dressed and spending the next two hours polishing his bloody car!'

Every so often, when Bill refused to pay her any money for the kids, she would go round to his house and let down all the tyres on his car. He knew who was responsible but would do nothing about it, pretending nothing had happened.

When the ex-wives of the SAS read that the Government was launching the Child Support Agency, forcing fathers to accept financial responsibility for their children, there were many very happy women in Hereford.

Because the SAS Ex-Wives Club was a force to be

reckoned with, there would be no chance of husbands persuading, coercing or frightening their former wives into not applying for child maintenance through the CSA.

Many believed that the introduction of the CSA would also make husbands, who might be contemplating ditching their wives, think twice before moving in with another woman, for now there would be no way that feckless, irresponsible SAS soldiers would be able to shirk their responsibilities.

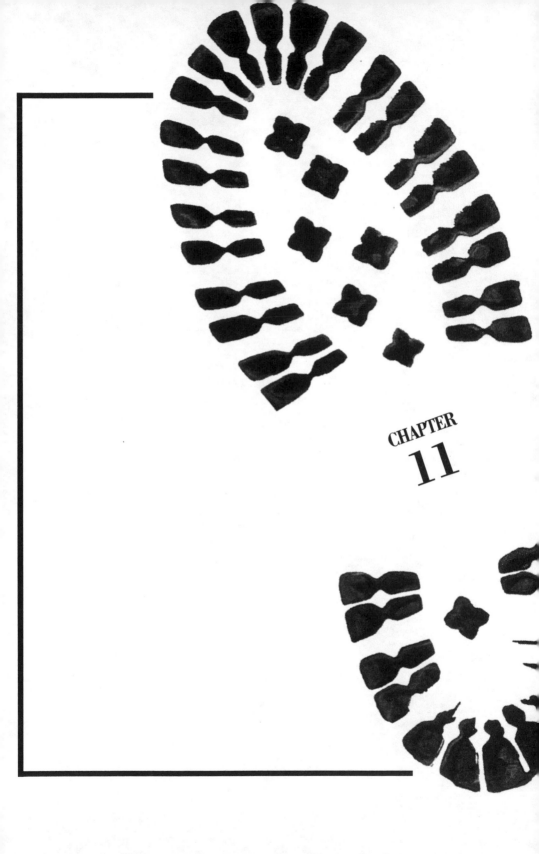

CHAPTER
11

'In carrying out an operation, each SAS man is exercising his own individual perception and judgement at full stretch.'

COLONEL DAVID STIRLING

TWO DAYS BEFORE LEAVING FOR THE GULF WAR, Andy came round to see me and Joanna as he did most days during the week. Ever since he had walked out five months previously, he would visit us most afternoons, calling at around 3.00pm and leaving two hours later. Andy loved coming to see Jo, who was then nearly four years old, and I would feel a warm glow watching them playing and fooling round together, especially when Andy tried to teach her how to play football in the back garden.

When indoors, Andy would spend most of the time

playing with Jo while still chatting away to me. Andy never stopped chatting. Indeed, he was known as a babbler throughout the Regiment, with some mates referring to him as a 'gobby git'. Nothing would stop Andy jabbering.

He would also spend much of the time talking to me about my future: where I should live; what I should do; and how I should look after Jo. But most conversations would end with him suggesting that I leave Hereford and go to live somewhere else, preferably near my parents. To me, however, it seemed defeatist to move back to Gosport, although part of me realised that would probably be the most sensible decision. I knew my mother would love to have Jo living so much closer. Selfishly, I also realised that if I found somewhere to live near my parents, I would lead a far freer life with permanent, willing babysitters close by.

I suppose that one of the reasons I didn't want to move from Hereford was the very fact that Andy was keen for me to go away. I wanted to reach my own decisions without him dictating my life for me.

Andy would urge me to sell our house and move into another smaller house, or, perhaps a flat. I would tell him that I had no intention of moving to a flat because I wanted a garden where Jo could play in safety. He understood that argument so he dropped the idea, but still pressured me to sell and move to a smaller house.

He urged me to leave my job and apply to the DSS, whom he presumed would not only pay the interest on the mortgage, but would also give me an allowance to feed and clothe Jo and pay all my household bills. But he was honest enough to say that such an arrangement would benefit him greatly, making it easier for him to make ends meet. He also hinted that when everything had been sorted out he would, of course, pay monthly maintenance for Jo. I didn't want to know about approaching the DSS, but I agreed to search for a smaller, cheaper house for Jo and me which would ease the repayments Andy was making on the mortgage.

I would find myself becoming annoyed at Andy's behaviour, taking me for granted whenever he visited us. He seemed to think he still lived with us, asking for a brew or a sandwich, happy for me to run around after him, caring for him, although he no longer lived with us.

Most of the time he would talk to me about my private life, asking if I was dating someone, wanting to know when I went out and where I would go. He wanted to know whether I was visiting pubs and clubs and most days he would warn me that people all over Hereford were telephoning him whenever they saw me out on the town.

He would tell me how hurt he was with people phoning him telling tales of seeing his wife out drinking and enjoying herself around Hereford. He would tell me that, in law, I was still his wife and that I should remember that on all occasions, never doing anything that might bring him into disrepute with his mates or, more importantly, with the Regiment.

One particular afternoon, however, we were chatting in the kitchen when the phone rang. It was my former boyfriend, Brian, the SAS man who had promised wedding bells and a life of bliss even though he happened to be married at the time. We had happened to meet a few days earlier and he asked if I would like to go to dinner one night, as he was then well and truly divorced.

'It's me, Brian,' he said, 'You remember that dinner date you promised? What about tonight?'

Andy, of course, was listening to every word and I rather enjoyed the fact that I was being asked for a date, the first time Andy had ever heard anyone ask me.

'Yes,' I said, jauntily, 'I'd love to go. If I can't arrange a babysitter, though, I'll have to ring you back.'

I was confident that my friend Lynn would happily look after Jo. She had two boys and a girl and Jo enjoyed staying with them overnight.

'Who was that?' Andy asked casually

I didn't say a word, but I wasn't sure whether he knew if the caller was a man or a woman. He never mentioned the phone call again.

I was feeling confident and for the first time I asked Andy if he would mind leaving as I wanted to take a shower and pack an overnight case for Jo before my dinner date. He didn't like the idea of being pushed out of the house, but he seemed to accept it readily enough.

Sometime after 1.00am I was upstairs in the bedroom enjoying a bottle of red wine with Brian. I had laughed and relaxed that evening with Brian, recalling old times and, for a few hours, forgetting my problems.

I had taken a bath and was wearing a nightdress and dressing-gown and Brian was fully clothed. He had asked if he could stay the night in Jo's room, but I felt sure that he wouldn't have stayed there all night.

Suddenly there was a knock at the door.

Brian and I looked at each other.

'Who the hell can that be?' I wondered and went to the window. I could see the top of Andy's head.

'It's Andy. You had better stay there,' I said to Brian, 'I'll sort it out.'

The moment I opened the door, Andy strode in. 'I want to talk to you,' he said, walking into the lounge and sitting down.

I sat on one sofa and he sat on the other. 'What the hell do you want to talk to me about at 1 o'clock in the morning?' I said, somewhat exasperated.

'Where's Jo?' he asked.

'She's being taken care of,' I replied.

'I must talk to you,' he repeated, 'I'm off to the Gulf in 48 hours.'

'So?' I asked, 'Why have you come round here now, at this time? Did your girlfriend kick you out, or something?'

He did not reply, and I would never find out why Andy came round that night.

As he was about to answer, we heard a creak upstairs as though someone was walking around. Andy looked at me for a split second and then leapt from the sofa and ran upstairs shouting, 'You've got someone up there.'

Within five seconds, Andy was running back down again, confronting me as I stood motionless, not daring to move. Seconds later, Brian came downstairs and stood watching us as the row developed.

'Why him?' he said, his face inches away from mine. 'Why him?'

Andy continued: 'This is my house ... I put everything into this house ... We built this fucking house together ... and you invite him back here ... why him, for fuck's sake, why him?'

'For Christ's sake, Andy,' I shouted back, 'you've probably just come from Jilly's bed. You seem to have forgotten that you left this house five months ago. You don't live here any more.'

'Yes, but I pay the fucking mortgage and don't you ever forget it.' He walked out of the house without saying another word, leaving the front door wide open.

Throughout the drama Brian had not uttered a word, but had stood there watching everything. 'I think I had better leave,' he said. 'If you're sure you're going to be OK, then I think I had better go, but if you think he will return I'll happily stay.'

'No, I'll be fine,' I told him, 'he meant me no harm. In any case, I don't think he'll return tonight.'

'It's amazing,' he said before leaving, 'I hadn't even kissed you or touched you, but everyone always thinks the worst.'

With a smile and a look of resignation on his face, he said, 'Well, thanks for a lovely evening.'

Seconds after Brian had walked out, the phone rang. It was my father.

'Who have you got in that house?' were his first words.

'Nobody, Dad,' I replied truthfully.

'Well,' he said, 'we have just had a very irate Andy

McNab on the phone telling us that he has just walked into your house while you were in bed with Brian Pagnall.'

'Oh no,' I replied, realising the picture Andy had painted.

'Where's Jo?' my father asked.

'She's with a babysitter. She's fine.'

'Are you sure there's nobody in that house?'

Now I was becoming annoyed that my father didn't believe me. I was also angry that he had not even bothered to ask me for my side of the story.

'No, Dad,' I said, with more emphasis in my voice, 'there's no one here. I've just told you that.'

'Alright,' he said, 'we'll talk in the morning.'

I went to bed feeling angry, frustrated and fed up with the world. I seemed to have no one to whom I could talk, and now not even my parents seemed to want to believe me or take my side.

When I awoke the following morning the radio news bulletin was full of the threat of war in the Gulf and I thought how awful it was that Andy and I had fought when he was about to go to war.

The wives, as well as their SAS husbands, had been following the news bulletins from the Gulf with ever-increasing interest. It had been nearly ten years since the SAS had been involved in the Falklands War and all wives knew that their husbands were keen to play an active rôle in the battle to free Kuwait from Saddam Hussein's occupying forces.

Two SAS Squadrons were trained specifically for desert operations and we knew they would be the first to be despatched. Of course, we had heard the rumours and gossip emanating from Stirling Lines and we knew that some SAS troops had already been deployed both in Kuwait and parts of southern and western Iraq.

We understood that they had been engaged, with Special Forces from the United States, for several months, gathering information behind the enemy lines which would be of immense use to the Central Command planning the invasion of the occupied areas.

Everyone at Hereford had been thrilled to learn that General Sir Peter de la Billière, a former SAS Commander, had been appointed the Senior British Commander who would work closely with US General Norman Schwarzkopf.

Although Schwarzkopf was understood to be suspicious of Special Operations, the very fact that SAS troops had already been deployed made those still in camp at Hereford believe they, too, would eventually join the action.

G Squadron had been sent to the Gulf within weeks of Saddam Hussein's invasion of Kuwait in August 1990. And I had heard that at least one other Squadron was undergoing desert training, expecting to be air-lifted to the Middle East at a moment's notice. Despite the secrecy that surrounds the Regiment, all the wives, as well as ex-wives, would know whenever any SAS troops were to be sent overseas.

As Christmas and the New Year passed, there were a number of SAS men fearful that they might not be called for duty in the Gulf. They all knew that the SAS would have wanted to send three of their four Squadrons, always leaving one back home to cover emergencies that might arise somewhere else in the world. But no one wanted to be in the Squadron left behind at Hereford.

The morning following Andy's outburst over Brian, there was a letter on the doormat with no postage stamp, so it was obvious that Andy had taken the trouble to hand-deliver the note before flying off to Saudi Arabia.

His letter both saddened and surprised me. He asked me that if he should die in the Gulf War, I must tell Joanna how much her father had loved her and how much he had adored her. He asked me to sustain his memory so that Jo would never forget him.

But the letter, written erratically, was also a ferocious attack on me, describing me as a 'slut' and demanding that as the mother of his daughter I must change my ways and become a better mother to his child. The letter seemed full of anger and hate and I felt that through force of circumstances I had been responsible for Andy going off to war in an anxious state of mind. That upset and worried me during the months he was away.

He also announced that he felt 'totally and utterly justified' in leaving me as, he alleged, I had 'committed adultery'.

More importantly, Andy informed me in the letter that he had been advised by his solicitor to pay only half the mortgage repayments on our house.

I didn't in any way want to alarm Joanna to news of war and expose her to TV pictures of soldiers, the men in uniform who would look very similar to her beloved father. I therefore made sure that I listened to the radio news bulletins early in the morning and watched the TV news at night so I could catch up with what was happening in the Gulf. I thought, hopefully, that Joanna would be oblivious to the fact that her father was taking part in a full-scale war in some far distant land.

When the SAS is involved in any major mission, such as the Falklands, most wives adopt the same technique in an effort to shield their younger children from worrying about their fathers.

Despite this, Joanna would ask during the time Andy was away why he had stopped calling round each day to play with her, and I would tell her that he was away 'on exercise', not wanting to worry her. She was nearly four years old and as bright as the proverbial button, and I think she might have realised what war entailed. I just preferred to keep her innocent of the possibilities. I also realised that as the daughter of an SAS man, she would learn of war soon enough.

I would generally buy the *Daily Telegraph* because I hoped there would be more news of the war in a broadsheet than a tabloid newspaper. I would read every detail and would find myself picking up and reading other newspapers I came across and so, hopefully, finding out as much as possible about what was actually happening 'on the ground'.

I would lie awake at night thinking of Andy, wondering what he might be doing. I knew enough to understand that B Squadron 22 Regiment SAS would not be waiting for the ground attack to start, nor waiting to go in behind the tanks with the bulk of the infantry.

*　　　*　　　*

I had read books about the history of the SAS, including *Who Dares Wins*, the unofficial history of the Regiment by Tony Geraghty, detailing the Regiment's illustrious exploits from the very first SAS operations during the Second World War.

After the disaster of the first parachute operation, unwisely carried out in a vigorous sandstorm, a unit only 20 strong joined with men from the Long Range Desert Group and, by driving around North Africa, managed to destroy more than 100 Luftwaffe aircraft on the ground within a matter of weeks. Before the desert war was over, the SAS had destroyed 400 German aircraft and huge numbers of other weaponry.

I knew that David Stirling, a 6ft 5in-tall young Lieutenant, a Cambridge-educated Scots Guardsman, was the man who started it all. While in hospital recovering from a serious back injury, Stirling wrote a memo, in pencil, in which he argued that strategic raids — deep penetration raids behind enemy lines — did not require massive back-up.

He believed such a force, using parachutist saboteurs, could inflict a level of damage on enemy airfields equivalent to that of a Commando force 20 times greater. I learned that the organisation had earned its glittering reputation through its activities in Sicily, Italy, France, the Low Countries and finally Germany itself, throughout the Second World War.

The SAS was disbanded after 1945, but was hurriedly reformed again to tackle the Communist uprising in Malaya. The Regiment served from 1950 to 1959, and then for a further four years in the jungles of Borneo.

From there the SAS fought with great distinction in Oman and Saudi Arabia.

In the six years of intense guerrilla war in Oman, the Regiment only lost 12 men. But from 1969 onwards, more SAS men would become involved in the longest war they had ever known — patrolling and gathering intelligence in Northern Ireland.

But I had grown up with only one brief example of the SAS in action. I, too, would never forgot the TV news film showing an SAS counter-terrorist squad, dressed in black fatigues and gas marks, abseiling from the roof of the Iranian Embassy in London in May 1980, in a desperate bid to halt the murder of 21 innocent hostages. On that occasion they carried Heckler & Kock MP5 sub-machine-guns, which would become a favourite among SAS troops.

That single success, captured on television and seen across the world, brought a fresh enthusiasm amongst politicians and public alike for full support and funding for the Regiment, which had always shunned both publicity and medals. The lifting of the embassy siege had been the first time that the mysterious élite of the British Army had fought a battle on Britain's own doorstep.

As a result, when Argentina invaded the Falkland Islands in the South Atlantic two years later, the British public knew that the men from the SAS would be there to help win back the islands for Britain.

The battles to retake South Georgia and the Falklands were brilliant successes for the SAS. Though the Regiment suffered both dead and injured in fighting on land, the majority of SAS men were killed when a Sea King helicopter crashed in Falkland Sound. Those SAS men who took part in the Falklands campaign won the respect of all those who would later win the privilege of being badged.

Once again a maxim, which every SAS soldier knows to be true, was confirmed during that war: 'Train hard: fight easy'.

Everyone associated in any way with the Regiment knew that as the Gulf War approached, the SAS would be at the heart of the action, taking the greatest risks. And it seemed that one of the areas which could have a vital effect on the outcome of the war would be to destroy Saddam Hussein's favourite weapon, the Scud missile.

Much of the early newspaper coverage of the war involved the Scud missiles, and the papers were full of details. I learned that the Soviet-built missiles were 37 feet long with a range of between 100 and 175 miles, and that they were transported and fired on massive eight-wheel trailers that doubled as launch-pads.

I also learned that they were not very accurate, that they had none of the high-tech precision of the American cruise missiles which inflicted such widespread damage on Baghdad and Saddam Hussein's vital military installations.

And the more the radio and TV news bulletins highlighted the potential danger of the Scud missiles, the more I came to believe that putting those mobile missiles out of action would be the perfect job for the men of the SAS. I would discuss all these possibilities with my father, a Royal Naval officer throughout his life, and he agreed that demobilising those Scuds was a job cut out for the SAS and the American Special Forces.

I convinced myself that this was probably the task that Andy and his mates had been given and that worried me even more. I realised that would mean operating behind enemy lines. I knew that was the prime rôle of the Regiment, with much of their training concentrating on surviving and fighting deep within enemy territory. But I still worried.

It seemed that no one had any idea how many of the Scud missiles Saddam Hussein had purchased or built for his forces. Estimates varied widely and I remember listening to a TV programme in which the so-called experts obviously had little idea of the quantity or the destructive power of the Scud's warheads .

I lay awake at night, trying to envisage Andy and his mates making their way under cover of darkness to covert positions in the Iraqi desert, closing in on Scud missile sites, carrying out attacks against targets, before melting into the background, lying low and snatching a hard ration meal and a few hours' kip during the hours of daylight.

I studied reports of the weather conditions, wondering how Andy and the lads would be coping. Andy loved the heat and would tell me that he would always prefer operating in the warmth of a desert than the cold of Antartica. But I would read of how cold the deserts of Iraq became at night during January, and I imagined him trying to cope with the freezing temperatures.

I would wonder how he was coping with the hard rations, and it reminded me of the time Andy cooked me an SAS meal. It would bring a smile to my lips as I memorised my one and only hard tack dinner!

One morning during our happy times together, Andy told me before I left for work one day, 'I'm going to cook dinner for you tonight, Babe, so don't buy anything.'

'What are you going to cook?' I asked him.

'It's a surprise,' he replied, 'but I promise you it will be absolutely delicious.'

Andy had never been one to talk about cooking and had never shown any indication of wanting to play the chef, seemingly preferring to walk in most evenings and ask me what was for dinner. Andy had always been wonderful to care for because he was so undemanding. I knew that many Regiment men expected their meat, two veg and a pudding every night of the week. Andy would be perfectly happy with a cheese sandwich.

As I walked into the house that evening, the whole kitchen was full of steam, with clouds of it bellowing out into the lounge. He appeared out of the mist with a tea towel over his shoulder and big grin on his face.

'Hi, chick,' he said, clearly proud of his cooking prowess. 'Come and look what I've cooked.'

'Can I see anything at all in there?' I said, giving him a kiss before making my way to the stove.

The kitchen was covered in pots and pans. It seemed as though he had used every possible container we owned and the four rings were all in use. The pots were full of bubbling water — the source of all the steam — with a single aluminium foil packet in each one.

'You've timed it perfectly,' he said, 'it'll be ready in a minute.'

Andy had laid the table and had lit a candle and opened a bottle of wine. I offered to help but he would not hear of it. I was fascinated, so I watched as he snipped the corners of two of the packets, the main course, and oozed out the contents. The beef stew and dumplings not only smelt great, it tasted delicious. Ten minutes later, he dived back into the kitchen for the pudding, another appetising dish — spotted dick and custard.

I joked to him, 'I used to feel sorry for you lot when you were out on exercise surviving on hard rations. No more, mate, that was lovely.'

My treat wasn't over yet. 'I'm even going to do the washing up,' he announced proudly, as though sacrificing himself to hours in the kitchen. He was back in three minutes. 'It's wonderful stuff, eating hard rations. There's virtually no washing up.'

I would often think of the good times we shared together during the months he was in the Gulf. Despite the fact that we had broken up six months earlier, he would visit us each day so that although we would sometimes bicker and argue, I would see him and a sort of tortuous, uneasy relationship developed. But now he was away and in a dangerous war situation, the heartache and the arguments were forgotten and I somehow only remembered the good times.

They were uppermost in my mind whenever Jo and I would go for a walk together, or play in the garden — I couldn't help but think about Andy's visits to see Jo. One of his favourite walks would be to Queen's Wood on the outskirts of Hereford, and during the Gulf War I would take Jo there and play the games Andy had played with her. She would talk about 'Daddy' and the games he had played with her and, occasionally, I would feel a lump come to my throat.

Part of me would be angry towards Andy for walking out on us, but part of me could not help being deeply concerned for him and I would worry about what would happen to Jo if he didn't make it back. I didn't want her to grow up without her father around.

We received only one letter from Andy during his months away. It arrived only a few days after he flew to Saudi Arabia, so he probably wrote it either during the flight or shortly after his arrival. I hoped it would be positive and up-beat, but once again it seemed to be more of an attack on me and what he mistakenly believed was my life of sin.

He asked me not to write to him during the time he would be in the Gulf and that upset me. His letter ended with the words 'Give Jo a kiss'. When I had been feeling so positive and concerned for Andy, his letter left me feeling empty and sad that he should be thinking in that vein when he was flying into a war zone. I screwed it up and threw it away.

Rumours circulating around the camp throughout January and February involved the search and destruction of the Scuds and their TELs — transporter-erector-launchers. We learned that the SAS had been sent into the western Iraqi desert and US Special Forces had dealt with eastern Iraq. We also learned that both the

SAS and the Americans would locate the Scuds and then signal attacking US aircraft, mainly A10 and F-15s, enabling pin-point accuracy.

What we never knew, however, was whether any of our troops had been captured or, worse still, killed in action.

'Have you heard anything?' was the question on everyone's lips during those weeks when we waited for news to come through.

Every scrap of rumour and information would be sifted, analysed and spread throughout the camp on the wives' unofficial grapevine. Everyone would become involved in trying to determine what was going on. We knew that for much of the time, the SAS were involved in exercises overseas, not in full-scale wars against leaders like Saddam Hussein who seemed happy to bomb, poison and annihilate his own people if, for one moment, he thought they were against him and his élitist regime.

What we didn't know is how he would react to soldiers captured behind enemy lines. But, understandably, we feared the worst.

I also feared the non-conventional arsenal of weapons Saddam Hussein had allegedly been building and experimenting with during the 1980s. I would read of his chemical, biological and possible nuclear weapons capabilities. I also understood that one of the principle targets of the allied forces would be the elimination of these weapons and the factories that produced them, to curtail Saddam's ability to intimidate the region in the future.

Once again I believed that the SAS might be called upon to search out these weapons factories and, maybe, become involved in daring missions to destroy them. I hoped not. I hoped that the RAF and the US Air Force would be left to bomb the hell out of such places for fear that noxious, deadly fumes could be leaked from destroying the factories where the weapons were manufactured.

I lay awake at night fearing the terrifying effects such fumes could have on Andy and his mates, as I had remembered seeing photographs of entire Iraqi villages where Saddam had used such weapons to poison his enemies. The pictures showed the corpses of men, women and children lying in the open, their homes standing untouched.

Those pictures had brought home to me the horror of such a war and the terrible effects chemical and biological warfare could have on the soldiers, even those wearing protective clothing and gas masks.

Many of the Hereford wives were worried by the huge bombing campaigns, agreed by the Joint Chiefs-of-Staff and ordered by General Schwarzkopf, which the TV news bulletins led us to believe were occurring round-the-clock during the first weeks of the war.

It wasn't that the air-war would not have a maximum effect on airfields, military sites, communications installations and Iraqi ground troops, but we feared that the bombs and cruise missiles falling on Baghdad itself might create hatred towards the allied forces on the ground, particularly special forces like the SAS.

We knew that that would not bode well if any of them were captured by local people, who had recently suffered death and injury from bombing raids, and who might decide to wreak their vengeance on a lone captive.

On 24 February 1991, when we heard US President George Bush announce that General Norman Schwarzkopf had been instructed 'to use all forces available, including ground forces, to eject the Iraqi army from Kuwait', we knew that the ground war had begun.

Back home in Hereford, we wondered what the start of the ground war would mean to the special forces working behind the lines in Iraq. We hoped they would be instructed to lie low or return to friendly territory, rather than being ordered to take a more active role destroying enemy installations and lines of communication. In reality, of course, we had not the slightest idea, but that would not stop us thinking, analysing and worrying about our men in the desert.

I was happy that I had heard nothing whatsoever from the camp at Hereford — it meant, hopefully, that no news was good news. I had convinced myself that if anything untoward had happened to Andy, whether he had been captured or killed in action, then I would have been officially informed.

During the short three-day duration of the ground war, all the Hereford wives were following the destruction of the fleeing Iraqi army. We had seen the dramatic TV photographs of the Kuwaiti oilfields being torched, the plumes of fire and heavy smoke billowing into the atmosphere, blotting out the sun.

Then we saw the extraordinary TV photographs of the Basra Road when US aircraft strafed and bombed the thousands of Iraqi troops fleeing north from Kuwait in a convoy of 1,000 vehicles, seeking the safety of Iraqi territory.

Waves of aircraft attacked the hopelessly vulnerable convoy and some would later describe the attack as a 'blood sport', the Iraqis caught like rabbits in a sack. At Hereford, most wives wondered what all the fuss was about.

We knew that our men would have been treated in exactly the same way if they had been caught in a trap. The enemy, which had invaded another country and had shot and hanged innocent Kuwaitis, were now paying the price.

We hoped that Desert Storm would be allowed to continue attacking the feared Republican Guard, Saddam Hussein's élite troops, destroying their tanks, artillery and weapons and rendering the force incapable of conducting the type of heinous acts they had carried out in the past. Most SAS wives were annoyed when we read that much of the Republican Guard had been allowed to escape although much of their equipment had been completely destroyed in air attacks. But not all. We felt that they should have been destroyed, once and for all, to prevent any future threat.

As a result, the news that President Bush declared a ceasefire on 4 March, was received with mixed feelings at camp. We were happy that this would put an end to the killing, happy that it would mean the return of our beloved menfolk, but a little annoyed that the troops on the ground, who had risked their lives confronting Saddam Hussein, had not been permitted to destroy all the enemy forces, that, effectively, they had not been allowed to finish the job.

I waited with growing anticipation, wondering how Andy and all our other friends had survived the war, praying none had been caught, wounded or, heaven forbid, killed. And yet we all knew it would be very unlikely if all the SAS troops would return safely. We were all too well aware that if any risks were to be taken then it would fall to the SAS and the US Special Forces to undertake those dangerous tasks.

I would listen to the news for any British casualties. At the back of my mind, however, I knew there was a distinct possibility that no SAS deaths in action would be announced by the Ministry of Defence because the Regiment always kept such deaths under wraps, never broadcasting abroad that the Regiment had suffered casualties.

Everyone associated with the Regiment understood that the immediate families were always the first to be notified when an SAS man had been captured, wounded or killed. Though on many occasions, rumours of someone's death would have been signalled unofficially around the camp and many people would have heard of the possible death before official announcements were made.

I knew that if anything had happened to Andy in the Gulf War I, as his wife, would be one of the first to be informed.

Once the end of the war had been officially

announced, everyone in Stirling Lines and the SAS housing estates behaved with remarkable patience and self-control, no matter how worried they may have been. Everyone seemed up-beat, looking forward to welcoming the men back home, though, in reality, most wives seemed on tenterhooks, listening, watching and waiting for news. Some wives coped by rushing around, keeping busy, tidying and washing, preparing for the return of their loved one. No one wanted to sit around and chat any more, because we all knew there was now no point in discussing possibilities.

A few worried, younger wives continued to gather to talk about their men, especially as stories began to emerge in the newspapers that some British troops had been captured and tortured by Iraqi troops and handed over to Saddam Hussein's henchmen for questioning. Those older wives with more experience told them to stop worrying about such possibilities, because many of the hyped tabloid newspaper stories usually turned out to be wildly inaccurate.

As Jane, a woman in her 30s whose SAS husband had fought in the Falklands campaign, told a group of younger wives, 'When there's a clamp-down on news by the military authorities, the newspapers have to find something to write about. They will have guessed that 22 SAS is involved and so they put two-and-two together. Take no notice of the rubbish you read, otherwise you will worry yourselves into an early grave.'

Although Andy had not been in a war situation since we had met, he had spent two years on detachment in Northern Ireland where, I figured, there was probably more chance of him being captured, tortured and killed than in a conventional desert war. During his time away, I would try to convince myself of that argument, but I had still worried throughout the period he was out of contact.

I expected to hear from Andy within a week or so of the official ending of the war. I thought there might be a letter or a phonecall, or I might hear from one of the other wives that the Squadron was on its way back home.

Two weeks passed and I became worried and fearful. It was while driving back home one day, having taken Jo for a walk in the woods, that I suddenly had a premonition something was wrong.

I had been dreaming of Andy at night, seeing him coming home in his fatigues, watching him pick up Jo and kiss and cuddle her and then go out and play with her, watching the happiness on Jo's face at seeing Daddy once again. Now I felt that something had happened to him, that something was wrong — but I had no reason to think that. No one had mentioned anything to me, no one had said anything. But I became worried and that worry distracted me.

Suddenly I saw a car coming towards me on the wrong side of the road. It was dusk and I had my lights on, but the other car didn't. I must have panicked, wondering what on earth the other car was doing. Then I realised that it was me who was at fault, that I had strayed over to the wrong side of the road. I wrenched the wheel and somehow managed to get the car back into the correct lane.

My heart was thumping and I started to sweat. The other driver screamed past, blaring his horn at me. I felt embarrassed that I had made such a stupid mistake, but angry that by allowing myself to daydream I had put Jo's life at risk.

Worried for Andy, I decided to go and see a psychic, a woman in her 40s with shoulder-length dark hair and extraordinarily long fingers — she seemed to be more of a pianist than a psychic. She welcomed me on the doorstep with a lovely, warm smile and I felt instantly at ease, though I only went to see her because I was as worried as hell. From the moment I walked into her house we had a rapport and got on really well together.

I was impressed from the beginning, because she told me that she only wanted me to pay her at the end of the reading, not at the beginning as most do. She told me that I was worried, something that didn't surprise me because she could probably sense it.

But then her reading became more intriguing. She told me that she saw a dark-haired man, in a small, square, squat room, and that the man was thinking of celebrations, with lots of balloons. She added that everything was going to be OK.

I told her that it was our little girl's birthday soon and she nodded. But she had no idea that I was the wife, or ex-wife, of an SAS man; she had no idea that my husband was away in the Gulf War or whether he was alive or dead. I didn't know when I went to see her whether Andy was alive and well and with his mates back in Saudi, wounded and dangerously ill in a hospital somewhere, or even dead, his body lying buried in an unmarked grave somewhere in the vast Iraqi desert. Yet when I left her and drove home, I felt a sense of relief, more sure than I had been before that Andy would be all right and soon back home in Hereford.

Some wives, hearing nothing official from the SAS, would go to see the Families' Officer, asking if there was any news of their husbands or any of the Regiment troops. Each time the SAS authorities would say they had nothing to report, but would inform the next of kin as soon as they heard any news. They would tell them that, as far as they knew, there had been no fatalities, but they could not be certain.

A few days after the end of the war, I decided to take the bull by the horns and go to see the Families' Officer, an SAS Major with a strong Scottish accent who always had a fresh, ruddy complexion. He was serving out his last few years in the Army.

'What can I do for you?' he asked cheerfully as I walked into his small office, beyond the main office which was staffed by two or three civilian secretaries. On one wall was a map showing all the SAS housing, street by street, with the names of every soldier written in small print by the house where he lived.

'I'm Mrs Andy McNab,' I said, sounding stupid.

'Yes, I know that,' he said, 'we've met before. How can I help?'

'I wanted to know if you had any news of him,' I said, 'because I've heard nothing, not a word.'

'There is nothing that I can tell you at this time,' the Major replied in a reassuring voice. 'All I can tell you is that we have had no reports of any fatalities. We are expecting a complete update on the condition of all our men within a matter of days. As soon as we hear anything, I will notify you.'

'Thanks,' I said, 'but have you any idea exactly when we might hear or when they might return home?'

'Not precisely,' he said, 'but there are reports that some Regiment troops may have been captured. But I cannot tell you the names of those men because not all of our Regiment troops have contacted us yet.'

I left feeling somewhat relieved because I felt that no news gave me hope that all would be well. It did at least make sense to me that not all the Regiment troops had been back in contact, especially if they had been spread across the length and breadth of Iraq.

I decided to pull myself together and to stop worrying about Andy. I could see the other wives encouraging each other to go out and have a drink, relax and stop worrying.

One day at a coffee morning I met Rosie, an SAS wife about my age, who had been married for two years with a baby daughter. She had also worried about her husband and had found it difficult to sleep at night, fearful that her husband had been killed or wounded. She persuaded me to stop fretting and go out and have a drink.

So we did. For the first hour or so, however, I felt embarrassed, worried that people were staring at me, as though condemning me for being in a pub and having a drink when my husband was away fighting a war in Iraq. Two stiff Bacardi and Cokes helped put everything in perspective and I began to relax and enjoy myself. We talked about everything that night, except about the Gulf and our husbands, because we knew that would probably make us both maudlin and miserable.

We would go out together again once or twice before I got the knock on my door.

It was the Scottish Major from the Families' Office at Stirling Lines.

'Can I come in?' he said, and his voice seemed strained as though he was trying to sound cheerful. My heart began to thump as I led him into the living-room and asked him to sit down.

'It's about Andy, isn't it?' I asked before he had time to sit.

'Yes, I'm afraid it is,' he said, his voice sounding doom-laden. 'I am afraid Andy is missing. 'Sometimes, things like this happen and you must prepare yourself for the worst.'

I suddenly didn't want to hear any more, for it seemed to me at that moment that Andy was probably dead and that this Officer was trying to let me down, slowly, preparing for the news that would inevitably come later — that Andy had been killed in action.

Then the tears began to roll down my cheeks. My defences had gone; the tension that I had felt for weeks and tried so hard to control had disappeared in a single moment. I thought of Jo and what I would say to her, and then I thought of Andy and hoped the end had been quick. I knew that he hated pain.

After a few moments, during which the Major kindly fetched me a glass of water, I found the strength to gather my thoughts.

'Have you any further news?' I asked.

'Not really,' he said. 'It's been five weeks since they went missing. We do fear that the worst has probably happened and we are thinking of visiting all relations and telling them what we know. We thought you should know.'

'Have you told his mother yet?' I asked.

'No,' he said, 'not yet. Why do you ask?'

'Because I don't think you should tell his mother until you are absolutely certain. She would be totally distraught by the news and would probably have difficulty coping. She is a very dear woman who worships Andy, she lives for her sons. I think perhaps you should wait until you know the facts.'

'Thank you,' he said, 'thank you for that. We will bear that in mind.'

'So you have no other news?' I asked, wanting him to tell me every tiny detail.

'No,' he said, 'I'm afraid not. But I assure you that as soon as we have any news, we will pass it on to you immediately.'

That night I met Rosie and some other girls as arranged, but now I had another reason to go out and socialise.

I needed to talk to someone about Andy and to see whether any other wives had been visited by the Families' Officer and had been given the same devastating news. I wanted to know the names of the other missing men to see whether they were members of Andy's Troop or in his Squadron.

Within a minute of getting together with Rosie and

two other wives, someone asked me, 'Have you heard the news?'

'Yes, I've heard,' I replied, 'it's terrible. Do you know how many are missing?'

'Missing?' the three of them said in unison.

I looked from one to the other, confused, suddenly fearing that they weren't missing, but dead.

'They're not missing,' Rosie said, 'they've been captured. We just heard.'

'But this very morning I was told that they were missing,' I said, 'they had no idea about Andy. No one said anything about him being captured.'

'It's all around camp,' someone said, 'it seems pretty certain.'

'How many?' I asked. 'How many have been captured?'

'We don't know,' Rosie said, 'but there were eight in the team.'

Someone went and bought me a double Bacardi and Coke and I drank it in one. My mind was spinning. I wondered what I would tell Jo and decided to tell her nothing until I knew more. Johnny Two-Combs, a very good friend of Andy's who had been in the Green Jackets with him, and with whom I had always had a good friendship, came up to us.

He just looked at me and saw that I was visibly distressed. 'You stop worrying,' he said. 'He's captured and he'll be back. You must stop worrying about him. We're geared to this sort of thing, remember.'

I felt like burying my head in his shoulder and crying, desperately needing someone to comfort me. The very fact that he was a Regiment man meant he was the perfect person to choose.

He bought me another Bacardi but I never drank it. As he put his arm round my shoulder I burst into tears, the weeks of waiting had become too much and now I knew he was alive I could not stop the tears.

'All I want, Johnny, is to see Andy again,' I sobbed. 'I don't mind even if he walks through that door on the arm of Jilly, all I want to know is that he's safe and well.'

'Come on,' he said, when I felt unable to stop the tears, 'I'll take you home.'

When we arrived home ten minutes later my parents were sitting outside in their car. I was thrilled to see them though I hadn't expected them until the following morning. It was an emotional reunion and I felt that I should try and be strong for my parents' sake.

'Coffee,' I said, trying to calm myself, 'what we need is strong coffee,' and they went and sat down in the living-room.

We talked for an hour and Johnny tried to keep us amused about the times he and Andy had enjoyed in the Green Jackets and some of their amusing exploits since joining the SAS. Johnny left and my Mum thought we should all try to get some sleep because there was no point in waiting up, hoping for news that would probably not arrive until the following day.

The following morning we listened to the news bulletins, but no mention would be made of the missing SAS troops. All we heard on the bulletins was about the RAF pilots who had been shot down over Iraqi territory.

A couple of days later there was another knock at the door. It was the Scottish Major again.

'He's alive,' is all he said with a big grin on his face. 'He's alive.'

'Does Jilly know?' I asked.

'Yes,' he said, 'she knows. She knew some five weeks ago.'

I looked at him, stunned. Jilly had known for five weeks that he was missing but the SAS had kept that information from me. I was still legally married to Andy; I was the mother of his daughter; there had been no talk whatsoever of divorce and the SAS had let me continue worrying for five weeks without saying a bloody word.

I discovered later that Andy had put Jilly's and his brother's names on his next-of-kin form, with the request that they should be informed if he was injured or killed. They were barred by the SAS from telling anyone else what had happened to him.

I was furious, absolutely steaming, not at Jilly but at the bloody SAS establishment who had decreed in their wisdom that I, the legal wife of one of their Sergeants, should not be told that my husband was missing in action!

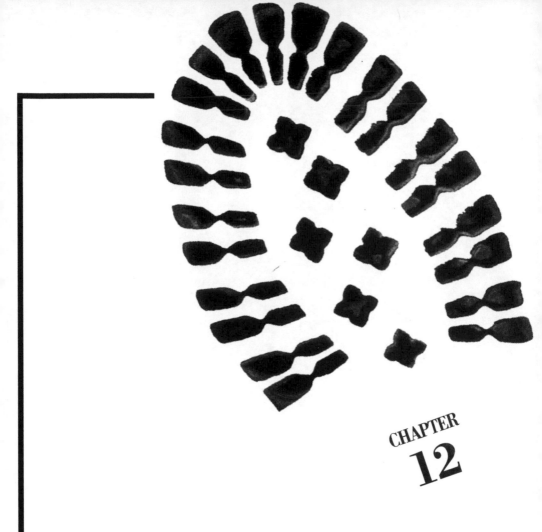

CHAPTER
12

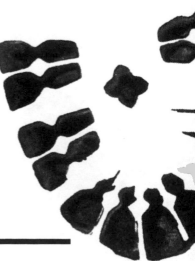

'In the SAS, each man is trained to a high level of proficiency.'

COLONEL DAVID STIRLING

THE FIRST DEFINITE NEWS I heard that Andy was safe and well was in a phonecall from his brother, John, during the first week of March. It had been two months since he had left Hereford.

He said, 'Fran, I've just received a phonecall from Andy. He's in Cyprus, in hospital. He sounds quite cheery. He told me that I am the only person he's called. He said that he didn't want to call Mum as she would have a fit. I just thought you would want to know.'

'Thanks very much,' I told him, 'that's great news, thanks for phoning.'

I walked straight into the lounge and told my father. 'Great news; that was John; he's just heard from Andy. He's in hospital in Cyprus and he sounds fine. I'm popping round to see Jilly to tell her the good news.'

As soon as Jilly opened the door I could tell she had already received a phonecall from Andy.

'Have you heard from Andy?' I asked.

'Yes,' she said, 'I heard from him a couple of days ago, as soon as he arrived in Cyprus.'

Once again I felt utterly foolish, stunned by news about Andy which I was again hearing second-hand. I felt deflated and somewhat humiliated.

'Oh good,' I said, the enthusiasm draining from my voice, 'that's fine then.'

As I walked down the path, Jilly shouted, 'How's little Jo?'

'She's fine, thank you,' I replied, in a resigned, reluctant voice, to remind Jilly that she had nothing whatsoever to do with Jo.

But she continued, oblivious to my mood, and cheerful in her moment of victory. 'I'll let Andy know she's fine when I speak to him. I'm expecting another call later tonight.'

I kicked myself all the way home. I had gone round to her house extending the hand of friendship, to let her know that Andy was alive and well and in hospital in Cyprus. And she had made me feel so very small.

I went back home and told my father what had happened.

'I feared that might happen,' he said. 'As soon as you left here I worried that he may have phoned her. You're just too soft, Frances. You must learn to toughen up.'

'I know, Dad,' I told him, 'but if she hadn't known then I would have felt awful in not telling her what I knew.'

I didn't know what to do or where to turn. I knew my father was talking sense and yet I didn't know whether I had the strength to go through with it. I knew I was no toughie and yet I found myself thinking that I must change. I hated being a doormat and yet I feared I would be one throughout my life. I wondered then that if I had been tougher, if I had fought dirty, perhaps I would still have been with Andy.

But he wanted to go and I let him go. I told myself that perhaps the time had finally arrived when I would start to become tough, play the whole bloody game like everyone else did, doing what they wanted and hang the consequences.

All day I wondered what to do. Then suddenly I had a great idea. I became convinced that Andy would phone me the forthcoming Saturday night, so I was determined that I would go out, get rip-roaring drunk and stay the night at a friend's house. I didn't want to talk to him; I didn't need to talk to him.

But what angered and upset me was the fact that he didn't seem to want to talk to Jo. The truth, I discovered later, was that he was unable to telephone Jo, because no one was supposed to know of his release. He did make arrangements to see Jo as soon as he returned.

I now knew that he was in good hands and recovering from his ordeal. Now I could cease worrying about Andy and begin thinking of my future relationship with him. I certainly didn't want Andy to think that I was sitting by the phone day and night, waiting for him to call. I was going out.

That Saturday night I drove to the Newmarket Tavern in Hereford market where I met two or three of my mates who were having a night on the town. 'Have a drink?' they asked as soon as I walked in.

'I'm having more than one,' I said, 'I need a dozen.'

They asked me why I was looking so angry and I told them what had happened.

'Good on you,' they chorused. 'The little bastard!'

I felt among friends again and I bought them all drinks. They were wonderful to me that night, cracking funny ex-husband jokes, boosting my ego and trying to help me forget how rotten the whole awful business had been.

As I drank I became maudlin, and began to think that I was behaving childishly, that I should rush home and wait for the phonecall I was convinced would come that night. But whenever my friends saw me looking depressed, they would talk to me, laugh, tell jokes and take the mickey out of the men hanging around the bar. Much later that night, I went home with Rosie and slept on her sofa.

When I awoke with a thick head the following morning, I phoned my mother. She did not sound pleased. 'Your husband called last night,' she told me, not asking where I was staying or how I felt.

'I knew he would,' I replied, 'what did he have to say?'

'He had a great deal to say,' she said, a warning tone

in her voice. 'I think you had better return home so that we can discuss the whole matter.'

Feeling awful, I drove home and my parents looked stoney-faced as I walked in and sat down. I feared the worst.

My mother told me that Andy had called that night and talked non-stop for more than 30 minutes.

She told me how shocked she had been with everything he had told her; how he knew for certain that I had had a number of affairs during our marriage; how he had caught me in bed with my old flame Brian Pagnall; how I would spend so much time out at night, drinking and partying; and how awful he had felt having to listen to camp gossip about his promiscuous wife's various affairs.

I let her tell the whole, sad, sorrowful and untruthful story without interruption. It was better to let her get it off her chest without a comment. When she had finished, I said, 'Mum, that's all rubbish. You know that I never had an affair while we were together. Never.'

'What I do know,' she replied, accusingly, 'is that you stayed out all last night. Where did you stay?'

'Mum,' I replied, 'I stayed with a friend. Her name's Rosie. Phone her if you don't believe me.'

'Andy told me that he had proof of your affairs,' she said.

'What proof?' I asked.

'He told me that he had seen letters from one of your girlfriends,' she said. 'She was writing to her boyfriend in the Gulf. She wrote that she was worried about you because you were going out so much. He even told me that he would bring the letters and show me.'

I didn't know what I could say to my parents to make them believe that I was telling them the truth, that everything they had heard from Andy the previous night was a load of rubbish, nonsense and lies. I knew that in their eyes I didn't look very convincing, sitting in front of them obviously suffering from a hangover and having spent the night away from home.

'It is up to you whom you believe,' I told them, 'but I can promise you that I never had a single affair when Andy and I were together. If you want, I will swear that on the Holy Bible.'

I knew that Andy had no proof of any affairs. He couldn't have. I knew the game he was playing, suggesting that the only reason he had left me and Jo for another woman was because of my constant infidelities, and that I, not Andy, was responsible for the breakdown of our marriage.

My mother would tell me later that when Andy drove down to Gosport to visit my parents when he returned to England, she asked him whether he had brought the letters, the proof of my infidelity. He told her the letters had been lost. She would never be shown any such letters.

Waiting for Andy to return home to Hereford would be a nerve-wracking experience. I wanted to see him, to see how he had managed to cope with the imprisonment, the torture and the beatings that we had heard about. We had seen the photographs taken in captivity of the two RAF fliers who had ejected from their Tornadoes over Iraq and how they looked.

I had watched them on TV when they were paraded for the world to see, their faces covered in heavy bruising, their eyes hardly visible. It was their demeanour that worried me, for both men seemed as though they weren't sure what they were saying, what they were doing or even where they were.

Those horrific TV pictures were the talk of the wives at Hereford for days, as we all feared the punishment that would be meted out to SAS personnel if they were caught operating behind enemy lines.

It was the photograph of the RAF fliers which so alarmed the wives. SAS wives are meant to be tough, they are believed to be hardened to the dangers to which their men are exposed, because they know their husbands thrive on danger and risk-taking. It's not true. In public, some may try to hide their feelings, but in private they are as vulnerable and nervous as any wives seeing their loved one go off to war.

I could tell looking at the anxious faces of the wives that, from the nervousness they portrayed at that time, the womenfolk of the SAS do indeed suffer great anxiety and trauma when they feel their men are in real danger.

I would listen to a number of SAS wives at this time, all anxiously waiting for their men to come home, not knowing whether they would be returned to Hereford in a black body-bag or 'casevaced' on a stretcher into Brize Norton. They might be walking wounded or, please God, they could walk through the front door as if returning from nothing more strenuous than a forced march across the Brecon Beacons.

'They think it doesn't effect us,' Gillian said, the tears

welling in her eyes. A Newcastle girl of 24, Gillian sat at home nervously twisting her handkerchief as she talked of her fears. Her great friend Paula was with her, another young SAS wife whose husband had never seen a shot fired in anger before the Gulf War and she also wanted to talk.

'He went off in January so happy,' Paula said. 'I could see the adrenalin was flowing and he was hyped up. He couldn't wait to get to Saudi Arabia. He had been talking about it for weeks, wondering if the Regiment would be joining Desert Storm and hoping that his Squadron would be sent.

'I tried not to let on. I tried to be brave but in my heart I didn't want him to go. I would sit and watch Saddam Hussein on television during the news bulletins and I thought what an evil man he looked; I wouldn't trust him an inch.

'I could see that Jim wanted to go, sitting on the edge of the sofa watching the build-up night after night, punching the palm of his hand with his fist, eager to go.'

Gillian told me how she would sit at home during the day, waiting for the telephone to ring in case her husband phoned. She would wait for the post each morning hoping he had written. 'It wasn't the fact that I had heard from him,' she explained, 'but I knew that if I received a call or a letter it meant that he wasn't actually at war or messing about in the desert somewhere.'

Paula said that from the time her husband had left Britain to the moment she heard his voice at the end of the phone after the war was over, she had only slept fitfully at night. Working in a food factory from early in the morning until 2.00pm she would arrive home, sit down and fall asleep for an hour or more.

'It was the nights I couldn't take,' she said. 'I would watch a film on TV, or anything, until I felt drowsy and on the edge of falling asleep. I would have a drink of cocoa and go to bed. But, though exhausted, I would find it impossible to sleep. I would toss and turn and think of Billy out there in the desert being hunted by Iraqi troops. It was awful.

'I think it was the TV news that made the whole war so horrible for us wives. It somehow brought the reality of war into our living-rooms, into our lives, and I felt a part of the whole awful business. And of course that made me worry for Bill's safety.'

Trying to make light of the war, another SAS wife, Liz, the mother of two young sons whose husband had been in the Regiment only nine months, said that she had adopted the opposite technique of getting to sleep each night.

'When I had tucked the boys up in bed each night,' she said, 'I would come downstairs, cook a pizza or something easy, and sit drinking a bottle of red wine while I watched the telly. Some nights it worked,' she laughed, 'but sometimes I would stay awake until 3.00am worrying about him and what I would do with two boys and no husband if he didn't make it back.

'But don't let any SAS wife tell you that she doesn't worry about her husband when he's on a mission,' she said, 'we all do ... every one of us.'

The three wives knew that Andy had left me and had

gone to live with his girlfriend, and therefore, to all intents and purposes, I was an ex-wife.

I would tell them, 'I worry, too. I try to tell myself that it's different being an 'ex', but it isn't; not when you're the mother of his child. In some ways it's worse because you feel an outsider with all the fear and responsibilities of being a wife.

'And yet I can tell you that I've experienced exactly the same feelings as all of you have. The fear, the anguish, the distress of not knowing whether he would return or not. It's really no different.'

I waited with butterflies in my stomach when I knew Andy would be coming round to visit Jo and me. He had visited Jo when my mother was looking after her and then phoned to say he would call round, as usual, the following afternoon when Jo returned from school. I wondered how badly he had been beaten by the Iraqis, whether he had been tortured, and how he had managed to cope.

Of course I had heard rumours, but nothing more, of what had happened to the SAS men caught behind the lines.

I saw him walking, quite jauntily, up the path and ran to open the door with Jo by my side.

He picked her up and kissed and held her and Jo hugged him.

'Daddy, Daddy,' she said, 'you're home. Are you coming to play with me?'

'Yes of course I am,' he said, 'How are you? What have you been doing?'

He looked at me as he walked inside with Jo and

I saw no warmth in his eyes.

And yet, in that instant of seeing him, all my negative thoughts of Andy disappeared immediately. He looked slim, as though he had lost a little weight. I noted he was dressed in the brown leather jacket I had bought him as a Christmas present two years earlier.

As he sat on the sofa playing with Jo and chatting away, I realised that I still fancied him, that I still loved him, and I wished that he had come home from the war to Jo and to me.

But his voice and his eyes were cold, lacking any warmth and devoid of any love. That hurt.

He asked me whom I had been seeing, whom I had been dating. His voice was accusing and, I felt, filled with scorn and even a touch of loathing. That hurt, too.

His accusations and his attitude, however, made me put everything into perspective and forget my selfish feelings of sexual interest in the man who had been home for several days but only now had decided to come and visit the daughter he professed to love above all else.

I offered him a cup of tea because I wanted to escape to the sanctuary of the kitchen to think things through, to decide how I felt about this man whom I had loved so much but had managed, during the past few months, to convince myself that I was better off without.

I handed Andy his tea and asked if he wanted a biscuit. He looked at me and replied 'no', but Jo had heard my offer and she looked at me and, at the same moment, I saw two pairs of bright blue eyes looking at me and I realised how alike they were, especially their shape and colour.

Seeing likenesses like that frightened me, because I realised that Jo and Andy belonged to each other, in the same way as I realised that, despite what had happened, the three of us belonged together. But on that first day back together I also realised that Andy, no matter how much he loved Jo, wanted nothing whatsoever to do with me.

Out of the blue he turned, looked at me with those bewitching eyes and said, 'I thought about you a lot when I was captured, Fran. I thought, maybe, that I should come back, but then I knew that since I left, you had been seeing Brian and saw no point in it.'

I knew then that Andy was playing one of his favourite mind games, discussing what he might do but, in reality, having not the slightest intention of carrying out his idle thoughts. I knew that he had no inclination of returning to me and he realised that I knew it. I wasn't prepared to let him continue with that particular conversation, intriguing me with throw-away lines, hoping I would bite and become keen so that he could then throw it all back in my face.

I decided to change the subject.

'I heard you were tortured,' I said, sounding and feeling deliberately concerned for I had prayed that they wouldn't touch him.

'Yeah,' he replied, 'that's right. They used to light their cigarettes, puffing away in front of me. Then, when the cigarette was nearly finished, they would casually stub the lighted butts out on my thighs, making sure they kept the pressure on till the stubs were dead. Others stubbed their fags out on my neck.'

I winced and looked at his trousered legs, wondering how badly his legs had been burned, how often those bastard Iraqis had stubbed out their fags on his legs, and worried how he had managed to cope with the burning pain and the smell of burning hair and flesh.

I wondered how he had coped every time a guard lit another cigarette, knowing that in a few minutes the torture would start again, as another butt was stubbed out.

He told of the repeated beatings he received, bent over tables and flogged and kicked and punched by teams of soldiers, jailers and interrogators, who seemed determined to inflict as much pain as possible on their defenceless victim. But the torture would become more intense as his inquisitors demanded that he give them details of the Squadron's mission behind Iraqi lines.

He continued, 'They seemed to take pleasure in kicking my kidneys.' He put his hands to the small of his back, gingerly feeling his bruised and battered body, wincing as he applied a little pressure.

'As I lay on the floor, my hands and my feet bound together, they would come up to me, one after the other, aiming deliberately at my kidneys, smashing their heavy army boots into my back.'

Trying to sound matter-of-fact, Andy went on, 'Now my kidneys are split and I'll need an operation to ensure they will be OK in the future.'

I felt sick. I wanted to rush to the loo to be ill but Andy hadn't finished yet.

'And then my teeth ...' he went on. He put his hands to his cheek bones and my stomach churned. I wondered what they had done.

'They smashed out my back teeth with the butts of their rifles,' he said. 'I kept passing out with the pain. I was sitting on a chair blindfolded and my wrists were cuffed, and if I didn't give the right answer to their questions, someone standing behind me would smash the rifle butt into the side of my face, breaking my teeth.'

I shuddered at the thought of such excruciating pain and the heroic bravery Andy had shown.

'How did you cope?' I said to him, looking into his eyes and wondering how the hell anyone managed during such appalling torture to retain their sanity and powers of reasoning. I knew that if the Iraqis had done that to my teeth, I would have fainted within seconds and given them whatever information they required. But here was Andy, the man I loved, telling me quite casually how he had been repeatedly tortured in the most gruesome way, but managed somehow to be unaffected by the horrendous ordeal.

I wondered how he had the raw courage to cope with such atrocities and then be able to talk to me about them as if he was detailing what had happened to someone else, rather than to him. I realised then how brave and courageous he must have been, and I chastised myself for every nasty thought I had ever conceived about him.

I noted how Andy kept rubbing his hands together and I asked if anything was the matter.

'I still think I've got reverse feeling in my hands and my feet,' he said. 'They bound my hands and feet together so tightly that I lost all feeling. Then I suffered reverse feeling and that takes ages to go away. I'm rubbing them thinking I'm bringing back the circulation but actually they're fine. It's simply a nervous reaction.'

Andy told me that when the SAS lads had been released they had been flown to Saudi Arabia and then on to Cyprus. He told me that medical checks there revealed he was suffering from hepatitis. Other checks showed a dislocated shoulder, ruptured muscles in his back, scar tissue on both kidneys, burns on his thighs and loss of dexterity in both hands.

I looked into his eyes again and they seemed vacant, as though he was going through the motions but was hardly with us in the room. I wondered how deep the psychological scars had gone and wondered how long it would take for him to recover, how long it would be before Andy returned to his old chatty self, full of life and bonhomie and wanting to play enthusiastically with his darling Jo as he had always done.

As he talked to me and told me details of the truly horrific torture, imprisonment and deprivation he had had to endure for so many weeks, I felt full of sadness and pity for him. I also felt terribly guilty as though I was in some way to blame for the awesome atrocities he had had to endure.

'Listen, Andy,' I said to him, 'if ever you want to talk to anyone about what happened, please just come round and talk to me if you want to.'

He looked me full in the face.

'Why the hell would I want to talk to you?' he said, almost spitting out the words, and he turned to look at Jo, ignoring me and making me feel unwanted and useless and someone of no consequence in his life.

He left shortly afterwards and Jo and I went to the window to watch him drive away. We waved but he never turned to see if we were there and drove away.

*   *   *

Ever since Andy had let me know in the summer of 1990 that he wanted nothing more to do with me, I had waited and hoped, and sometimes prayed, that he would come back to Jo and me and give our marriage one more chance. I would never know the real reason why Andy had left us, and would blame myself as well as believing that, like many young men, he believed the grass was greener elsewhere.

In many ways I had been surprised that he had left us because of his obvious love for Jo. Whenever they were together during the years we were happily involved, Andy had been a marvellous, doting father, never happier than when playing with his little daughter or feeding or bathing her, making her smile and laugh. They seemed to adore each other.

Somehow I had survived those months of anger and wilful indiscretions, when I had assumed desperately, yet foolishly, that wild sex would assuage my feeling of emotional insecurity and low self-esteem. Now, I had buried myself in a job I loved, my responsibility in life, caring for Jo, spoiling her, giving her as much emotional support and love as possible. And by doing so I had settled down and found life far easier to cope with than I ever imagined possible when

Andy walked out of my life.

I had believed that my need for love, for a man, for sexual gratification had gone, vanished. I would enjoy the odd night out with other ex-wives and I still felt invigorated by the buzz of life around Hereford, engendered I must admit, by the knowledge that the men of the SAS made the town feel alive. And although I was no longer a part of the mystique I still felt a fulfilled person, not missing the tension, the fervent exhilaration, yet happily enjoying a wonderful life watching Jo grow up, going to school and making friends.

And my friend Nigel had made me realise that there were kind men in the world, men who didn't need to live the macho life, who didn't need to prove themselves, day in, day out, week in, week out, to their mates, their bosses, their women and to themselves. He had also made me realise that I didn't need the high-pressure excitement, the stimulation nor the constant buzz of camp life to make my life happy.

Nigel and I would see more of each other and, naturally, I would see less of my SAS friends, the wives and ex-wives who had been my best pals for years and who had helped me over my crisis. I began to trust him and believed that I was falling in love.

We would go for long drives in the country together, and find out-of-the-way country pubs I never knew existed around Hereford. He would love to walk down country lanes, just holding hands, listening to the wind in the trees and the birds twittering away. He taught me the names of so many wild flowers and trees, and the names of birds we heard but couldn't see.

He loved the outdoor life, enjoyed sleeping outside and he kept a small tent in the boot of his car. We would go off together for weekends, pitching the tent in some field, cooking a meal on an open wood fire, snuggling down in a sleeping bag, listening to the nightlife and making love under the stars.

I had never experienced such a life before and I enjoyed it enormously. It was a world apart from the swish hotels, four-poster beds and expensive dinners that I had always dreamed of as the perfect romantic weekend.

Most of the time, Nigel would question me about my life, my married life, Andy and the break-up. And I told him that, technically, Andy and I were still married, but in name only. I told him about Jilly and how, when Andy was in Hereford, he would visit Jo and me most afternoons to see his daughter and play with her for a couple of hours.

He told me that he had only recently moved to Hereford from the north of England and had left behind a girlfriend, Wendy, whom he had been dating. 'Wendy is now a closed part of my life,' he told me, 'that's all behind me now.'

And I believed him.

I even believed him when he failed to turn up for a wonderful meal I had prepared and cooked for him on Valentine's Day in 1991, the first time he had been invited to my house for a meal. We had arranged for him to arrive at 7.30pm and the dinner was cooking gently, the wine was open and the candles lit. Jo had gone across the road to stay the night with a friend.

When 8.30pm arrived, I began trying to phone his mobile number but it was permanently engaged. Then, at around 10.30pm his mobile finally rang. Before I had time to speak, however, the phone had gone dead. I went to bed, only to be awakened at 2.00am with Nigel apologising a thousand times for not being able to contact me, but saying that it was all to do with work. He would explain later.

The following night he came round and I tried to serve the belated dinner I had prepared so lovingly 24 hours earlier. Understandably, the dinner was no great success but the wine was fine and Nigel was wonderful, making love to me for three long hours.

A few days later my parents came to visit and they were sleeping in my bedroom. I had barely fallen asleep on the sofa downstairs when my mother wakened me, 'It's a friend called Nigel on the phone ... he wants to talk to you.'

Half asleep, I went to the phone and he sounded strangely different, a touch of desperation in his voice.

'Frances,' he said, 'I'm sorry to trouble you at this late hour, but could you come and see me, now. It's important. Can you drive to Sainsbury's car park? I'll be there.'

I glanced at my mother who gave me an old-fashioned look, as though she realised I was becoming involved in something deeper than a friendly flirtation. 'Thanks, Mum,' I said as I hurriedly pulled on some clothes and drove off to the rendezvous, full of anticipation.

From the tone of Nigel's voice I knew it couldn't be

good news, but I wasn't prepared for what would happen.

Nigel was sitting in the driver's seat of his black Porsche and a dark-haired young woman, whom I had never seen before, sat next to him. I parked my car and walked over to the passenger side of the Porsche. The door opened and the young woman, with a face like thunder, calmly got out and into the back seat, leaving me to sit next to Nigel.

As I shut the car door, I turned to Nigel. 'What the hell is going on?'

He had barely opened his mouth to reply when the woman behind us smacked him hard on the back of the head, 'Shut up,' she said, 'shut up.' And she hit him again.

'I think I had better explain,' the woman began. 'I'm Wendy, Nigel's fiancée.'

I turned and looked, first at her and then at Nigel, bewilderment and surprise all over my face.

'What?' I said, hardly able to believe what she was saying.

Nigel looked down at the steering wheel, sheepishly avoiding my eyes.

'I drove down from Scarborough earlier tonight,' she said, 'to find out what's been going on.'

Nigel turned to say something, but before he could say a single word, Wendy struck him again across the back of the head. 'Shut up,' she said, 'I've told you to shut up.' And she gave him another clout for good measure.

Wendy talked briefly of their relationship, telling me

that they had become engaged on Valentine's night, the same night that I had slaved over a cooker for Nigel and then fallen asleep waiting for him to turn up.

Nigel finally got a word in. 'We didn't get engaged that night,' he said, 'I told you it wasn't an engagement ring, just a ring.'

But Wendy hadn't finished yet. 'No, it might not have been an engagement ring exactly,' she said, 'because we had been engaged before and we had broken it off some months ago. But on Valentine's night you did give me a ring, we did drive to London, stay in a hotel and make love all night.'

Nigel looked totally embarrassed and I decided to leave and let the two of them sort out their relationship. I didn't want to know. I had heard enough.

A few minutes later, as I strolled aimlessly around and looked at the stars, wondering what on earth I would do with my life, I heard a car door slam and Wendy came up to me. She was a pretty girl, petite and attractive, standing only a little over 5ft tall.

As she approached, I felt a half-smile cross my lips, for this young woman had the guts to belt Nigel around the head, a strong, athletic man standing over 6ft tall and weighing over 12 stone.

'I'm sorry about this,' she said, 'but he's been kidding both of us. I have no bad feelings towards you, only towards that arsehole,' and she jerked her thumb over her shoulder towards Nigel still sitting silently in his car.

During the following few days, Nigel phoned two or three times saying how sorry he was and apologising for not telling me the truth beforehand. I was led to understand that Wendy had returned to Scarborough, having finally been told by Nigel that their relationship was over.

Nigel invited me out again and his protestations of love seemed more sincere than ever. Once again he hurried nothing, acting like the perfect officer and gentleman, until he realised I had forgiven him, if not forgotten the episode altogether. Once again he was wonderful in bed and our relationship seemed to be back on an even keel.

We began going on country drives again, making love under the stars and having a wonderful time together. It was while driving home one evening that Nigel's mobile phone rang.

'It's your father,' he said.

I took the phone, somewhat surprised.

'Yes?'

'What the hell do you think you are doing?' he began, his voice rising in volume. 'How dare you go gallivanting around the bloody country when your daughter is laid up in hospital.'

'What! What are you saying?' I stammered, unable to comprehend what the hell was going on.

'Phone your husband,' he thundered, 'phone him immediately. Do you understand?' and the phone went dead.

Shaking, nervous, unable to dial Andy's number, my mind was a blur, desperate to know what had happened to Jo. Nigel dialled the number and gave me the phone.

'Andy,' I yelled, when he picked up the phone, 'what's happened to Jo? Is she OK?'

But Andy didn't answer my questions. 'You lied to me,' he yelled down the phone, 'I had to phone your parents to find out where the hell you were. You left Jo with Jilly and me and went off not telling us where you were going.'

To keep the peace, I had previously told Andy I was going for a job interview. I knew he would have been upset if I had told him I was going off with Nigel.

'Andy, Andy,' I said, desperate to intervene and find out what had happened to Jo.

But he ignored my pleas. 'I tried your work, I even tried a couple of other places searching for you. No one knew where the fuck you were. Finally I contacted your parents and they told me you were out fucking someone. Where the hell are you?'

'I'm driving home now,' I said, 'but first tell me what has happened to Jo? Is she in hospital? What's the matter with her?'

Andy calmed down and told me that Jo had banged her head against a door at his house but nothing seemed wrong.

He went on, 'I took her to play school on the Monday morning, but a few hours later the school phoned to say she had vomited. I raced over and took her to the Casualty Department of the Hereford General. A doctor examined her and said she could have an ear infection which could have been exacerbated by the bang to her head. The doctor told me to take her to her GP.'

'So,' I said, 'how is she now?'

'She's fine,' he said, 'she's here, playing.'

I was perplexed. I wondered why my father had gone so berserk on the phone, telling me that Jo was in hospital.

Within seconds of ending the conversation with Andy, my father called back. He seemed far calmer.

'It seems,' he told me, 'that Jo is OK. Andy had told us that Jo had been admitted for an emergency operation which would entail her being kept in for at least seven days. That's why I phoned you.'

'I understand,' I told him, 'thanks for calling back. Now I understand what went on.'

But Nigel was far from happy. 'I can't take any more of this,' Nigel said. 'That man will never let you go. He will never give you a moment's peace because you are the mother of his baby. You can run and hide but he will always find you and drag you back again.'

We drove home in silence. As I got out of the car Nigel said, 'Let's cool it until you have your divorce ... then we'll see. OK?'

'OK,' I replied, but as I walked away from the car without looking back, I knew the relationship had come to an end.

I immediately called Andy and he told me that Jo was sound asleep and we agreed it would be better not to disturb her. He agreed to take her to school the following morning.

That night I lay on the bed and went to sleep not bothering to undress. I awoke at dawn, shivering, and ran a hot bath. I lay soaking for a long time and knew there was no point in continuing. I dressed in clean clothes and went to the medicine cabinet. I found some bottles containing paracetamol and some other tablets Andy had taken some time in the past. I filled a glass with water and went back to the bedroom. I sat on the bed facing the lovely photograph of Jo on the side-table and began slowly to put one tablet at a time in my mouth, swallowing each one. Then I started taking two at a time and then three at one go, washing them all down with water.

I felt no anger and no hatred, no distress and no sorrow. I just knew that I wanted to die, to escape all the pressures, to escape from Andy and his demands and tantrums and to escape the harsh judgements of my parents. There were no tears and I felt no anguish or remorse.

When I felt I had taken enough to kill myself, I picked up Jo's photograph and held it to my chest while I lay down waiting to die. But nothing happened and my mind began to work.

I thought of Jo.

The tears started to well in my eyes and then they began to flow. I began to sob, thinking what a selfish fucking bitch I was trying to kill myself and leaving Jo to fight all her own battles. She was only four years of age and I was leaving her, quitting, killing myself, just running away from life.

Then I thought of Jo being brought up by Andy and Jilly or maybe some other woman if he moved on again ... God, I had been Andy's third wife ... And he's still in his 20s ... How many more wives would he have? ... The lads already called him Henry the Eighth and I tried to remember how wives Henry had married ...

My idle thoughts were interrupted by the phone. I picked it up. It was Nigel.

'Just called to see if you were OK?' he said.

'I'm fine,' I lied, but suddenly my tears returned and he could hear me crying on the phone though I strained to stop. Suddenly I had a terrible fear I was going to die and that was the last thing I wanted now.

'What have you done?' Nigel shouted down the phone.

I couldn't find the strength to reply.

'Have you done something stupid?' he yelled again.

I was determined not to confess to Nigel what I had done, because I remembered that Wendy had told him that she had once overdosed during their relationship some years ago.

'Can you drive?' he asked, his voice a little calmer.

'Sure,' I said, trying to sound confident but feeling totally confused.

'Meet me at Sainsbury's car park in five minutes,' he said, 'I'll be there.'

As I drove up, Nigel was standing there waiting for me. As soon as he saw me, he realised what I had done.

'Now listen,' he said, 'you must tell me what you have taken and how many. Do you understand?'

I didn't reply but nodded my head.

'I've taken some paracetamol, lots of them and something else,' I said drowsily.

'You stupid bitch,' he said, trying to shock me, 'don't you know that paracetamol won't kill you ... it will just fuck up your body, your kidneys. We must get you to hospital.'

'I'll drive there now,' I said, 'I'll be fine. You go back to work. I can do this on my own. I want to.'

I didn't go to the hospital. Instead I drove home and phoned Gina, my Scottish girlfriend, whom I knew had overdosed some years before. She had taken so many pills that she had to be admitted to a mental hospital after suffering a complete breakdown.

'I need to see you,' I said. 'Can I come round for a cup of tea?'

Standing in her kitchen a few minutes later, I blurted out everything.

'Why?' she asked. 'You silly cow. What did you do that for?'

'I don't know,' I replied honestly, 'it just seemed the only thing to do.'

'Right,' she said, taking command, 'finish your tea ... you're coming with me.'

'Where are we going?' I asked stupidly.

'To hospital,' she replied. 'Like it or not, you're going to have your stomach pumped.'

Gina drove me to hospital and told them what had happened. I simply followed her until she handed me over to some nurses. They lay me on a bed and began to put this large, long tube down my throat. I fought them all the way.

At one point I remember two nurses holding me down while this young doctor began pushing the pipe down my throat. I couldn't take it and thought I was about to die. I vomited everywhere but they still continued. Eventually, after what seemed an age, they stopped and I felt like death.

I was taken to a ward and a doctor gave me an injection in my backside. The next thing I remember was waking up to see my parents staring down at me. I felt pathetic, useless and insignificant. I just wanted to cry, turn over and escape into sleep.

My parents told me that Gina had been a true friend, phoning them and telling them what had happened. She had also devised a plan to pick up Jo because she was convinced that if Andy discovered that I had overdosed he would refuse to hand Jo over. But she collected Jo and took her home until new arrangements could be made.

A couple of days later, I was allowed home and my parents came to stay for a short while until I felt strong enough to cope with Jo and my new situation.

Slowly, I regained my strength and my equilibrium and began to put my life into perspective. I vowed that I would never do anything so stupid as trying to commit suicide again, running away and leaving my darling Jo to cope with life on her own.

I knew my attempt at suicide had been foolish, stupid and selfish and each day I would castigate myself for having tried it.

But my relationship with Andy deteriorated more rapidly. It seemed to me that he really didn't like me and Jo staying around Hereford. It seemed to annoy him and his attitude towards me became more openly hostile.

Towards the end of 1991, I knew Jo and I would soon risk eviction from our home because Andy had stopped paying the mortgage and the arrears were climbing steadily. I had stopped work and we were surviving on social security, but the mortgage arrears were not being addressed and I feared the worst.

In early January 1992, I received a summons from the County Court. I was told the building society would ask for the formal repossession of the property and I was left in no doubt that the order would be granted.

I told Andy what had happened. He didn't seem too concerned. He believed I was looking for somewhere else to live, and that my father was helping me.

On January 24 my father came with me to attend the County Court hearing. He had considered paying the arrears and then helping me towards paying the mortgage, but the building society were adamant that they would enter into no new agreement until the £5,000 arrears had been paid. Understandably, my father was not prepared to pay that sum and so the repossession order was granted.

The following day my mother and I packed as quickly as possible and waited for the removal van to arrive. The earliest they could call was 11.30am the following morning and they arrived a little late. The men had barely begun taking furniture from the house when the bailiffs arrived.

Six men had driven up in three cars to see the eviction carried out, including the bailiffs and representatives from the building society.

'One o'clock,' an officious grey-haired man in a dark suit announced, 'one o'clock you must be out of here. And there's no argument. That's what it says on the court papers and that must be obeyed. Do you understand?'

'Yes,' I said, 'can't you see we are moving everything

as quickly as possible?'

'We've got another eviction in Abergavenny,' he said, as though speaking to everyone outside our little house, 'so get a move on.'

It soon became apparent that we would not have everything moved out of the house in time to meet the 1.00pm deadline, and the bailiffs began to walk up and down, urging everyone to work harder, worried in case they might be a few minutes late in completing their mission.

'If you blokes gave us a hand,' one of the removal men said to the group of six idle men, 'we might get this finished by one o'clock.'

None of them replied.

As the minutes ticked by, the removal men said that they could not possibly complete the job on time, so they suggested that they would move everything out of the house on to the front lawn and pack it in the van after the bailiffs had left.

'Right,' said one of the bailiffs, 'move everything on to the grass. We can't wait around any longer. It's nearly one o'clock.'

The removal men, helped by my mother and I, worked wonders. Thirty minutes later, having literally ripped out the last of the carpets, the job of emptying the house was complete. Without a word, the bailiffs stepped forward, slammed the door shut, taped the letter box and marched off to their waiting cars.

I felt angry, humiliated and deeply unhappy. All around me on the grass lay the remnants of my entire life. Everything I had striven for, worked for, loved and cherished was laid out before me for the whole world to gawp and stare at. Even Jo's toys were in a heap. At that moment I hated Andy McNab for everything he had done, but I had no strength left to fight. I sank to the grass and cried like a baby.

My mother came up immediately to console me. One of the removal men said, comfortingly, 'Don't worry, love, things will look better tomorrow.'

I had no wish to see tomorrow.

But somehow I found the strength to keep going, and watched disconsolately as the van drove away, taking all our furniture into storage. I had no idea when I would see it again.

A very good friend had agreed to let Jo and I stay at her house for a few days while our new home — a three-bedroom, detached, black and white Tudor-style house opposite where we were staying — was renovated. With part of the rent to be paid by social security and a very generous allowance from my father, I took over the lease. A month later, Jo and I moved in and began to build our home.

Some days before we moved, however, I received a letter from the DSS informing me that they had received a phonecall from my husband informing them that I was not providing properly for Joanna.

Apparently, Andy had complained that Jo was suffering from a rash and that her teeth were dirty. The letter went on to say, however, that from enquiries they had made, they believed that I was caring adequately for Joanna and were happy with the situation.

I was outraged that Andy would try to cause me so much trouble, and I wondered why he had acted in that way. I feared that he might, as some husbands do, be attempting to blacken my name with the authorities. Then, if he made a claim for custody of Joanna, his application would be seen in the light of a deeply worried husband trying to provide greater care and security for his child.

In my heart I could never imagine Andy stooping to such a low level, but I had to be prepared for any eventuality. I phoned the Social Services who assured me that they had found I was caring properly for Jo, but explained that they had to investigate all such complaints.

I decided to continue living in Hereford until Jo was five years old when she would start primary school. She had enjoyed play school and the nursery she attended, and seemed to enjoy school work, making friends and learning the alphabet.

I devoted myself to her but would, at weekends, join the ex-wives for a drink at a pub or a disco, relaxing but never drinking too much, chatting and catching up on the gossip. Sometimes I would find myself attracted to a man I saw, but not very often, and all the dances I accepted never led to more than a goodnight peck on the cheek.

I felt something would happen to alter my life but I had not the faintest idea what that would be. I wondered if I would throw myself into a new job when Jo began primary school, perhaps starting a business of my own. I doubted that I would ever meet another man who I would want to settle down with or even have little more than a fling.

One night in Garter's wine bar, I found myself and another ex-wife talking to two Americans visiting Hereford.

We talked and I found one in particular, a guy named John, a tall, well-built Master-Sergeant in his late 30s handsome and attractive. But it would be his gentleness that particularly attracted me to him.

In 20 seconds or less, I told him my history of Andy, of Jo and my life in Hereford.

'Why don't you come for a vacation?' he asked. 'You can bring Jo, have your own bedroom and no strings attached.'

'That would be fantastic,' I said, 'but are you sure?'

'Yes, I'm sure,' he told me. 'I'm also on my own, just like you. Only I haven't got a son or a daughter.'

Within weeks, we were talking every night on the phone. In August 1992, he paid for me to fly to America for a two-week vacation, and again in October.

As we walked and talked and enjoyed each other's company, John said to me, 'Listen, let's do something about this ... let's get married.'

I was amazed, taken back and not a little frightened. John was wonderful, everything a woman could possibly want in a man. He wanted me, wanted to care for me and love me and was happy to bring up Jo as though she was his own daughter.

I wondered if I should take such a gamble. In reality I hardly knew the man, although he had shown me nothing but love, concern, gentleness and kindness. And he had re-awakened my passion, wonderfully.

I took the gamble and we married the following July, three months after my divorce from Andy in 1993.

He had not been happy at the prospect of my taking Jo and going to live in the United States, but he had started to write his brilliant manuscript *Bravo Two Zero*, the book that detailed the story of his SAS patrol behind enemy lines in Iraq. His book would be received with fantastic acclaim and ecstatic reviews — the best account yet of the SAS in action — and his writing would make him a millionaire as well as securing his reputation as one of Britain's toughest and most heroic soldiers.

It also made his beloved Jo so proud to be his daughter.

POSTSCRIPT

FOLLOWING THE INCREDIBLE SUCCESS of *Bravo Two Zero*, in which Andy McNab recounted truly heroic exploits during the Gulf War of 1991, he wrote another best-seller, *Immediate Action*, the no-holds-barred account of his extraordinary life from the day he was found in a carrier bag on the steps of Guy's Hospital, to the day he went to fight in the Gulf War.

Immediate Action tells the story of McNab's wild youth and of his years with the SAS, serving at the centre of covert operations for nine years and on five continents.

After leaving the SAS in February 1993, Andy McNab has lived abroad.

He was invited to act as technical adviser on the highly successful Hollywood film *Heat*, starring Robert De Niro, Al Pacino and Val Kilmer.